ELDERS' TRAINING

THE VISION
OF THE
LORD'S RECOVERY

BOOK 2

WITNESS LEE

Living Stream Ministry
Anaheim, California

First Edition, 6,000 copies, December 1985.

Library of Congress Catalog
Card Number: 85-82044

ISBN 0-87083-114-3 (hardcover)
ISBN 0-87083-115-1 (softcover)

Published by

Living Stream Ministry
1853 W. Ball Road, P. O. Box 2121
Anaheim, CA 92804 U.S.A.

Printed in the United States of America

CONTENTS

FOREWORD

During February of 1984 over three hundred and fifty brothers from six continents gathered in Anaheim, California with Brother Witness Lee for a two week international elders' training. The messages that were released at that time are the contents of this four volume set. Book one presents the essential aspects of the ministry of the New Testament; book two sets forth the vision of the Lord's recovery; book three covers the way to carry out the vision; and book four emphasizes other crucial matters concerning the practice of the Lord's recovery.

Those of us that were in these meetings were deeply convicted of our need to be further enlightened by the Lord concerning God's economy and concerning the intrinsic essence of the New Testament ministry which is for the carrying out of this divine economy. As the Lord's recovery is continually spreading throughout the world, these messages are more than crucial and urgently needed. We believe that they will render a great help in preserving all the saints in the central lane of God's economy, without any deviation, for the fulfillment of His eternal plan. Our hope and expectation is that these messages will become a governing and controlling vision for all in the Lord's recovery. May we prayerfully consider all the points presented in these books and accept them without any preferences.

November, 1985   Benson Phillips
Irving, Texas

CHAPTER ONE

THE VISION CONCERNING GOD, CONCERNING THE FATHER, THE SON, AND THE SPIRIT, AND CONCERNING GOD'S ECONOMY

In the Lord's recovery we have received a particular vision which is absolutely based upon the divine revelation in God's New Testament ministry. It is not so easy to tell you what this vision is in full. In these chapters we could only summarize the crucial points of the vision the Lord has given to us in a very brief and concise way.

CONCERNING GOD

In the first place, we need to see what our vision is concerning God. God is triune. He is one, yet three; and He is three, but still one. He is three-one, and this Triune God is the Father, the Son, and the Spirit (Matt. 28:19). The Three coexist and coinhere. They are three, yet still one. They are distinct, and They are one. Our human mentality is altogether unable to grasp the mystery of the distinction of the Trinity in the Godhead and the oneness of the Trinity.

CONCERNING THE FATHER

Next we need to see what our vision is concerning the Father. The Father is the source. We need the realization of the Father as the source, though we do not need much explanation concerning this point. In addition, we need to see that even the Father Himself is triune, and He is triune not only in one way but in three ways. As to His Person, the Father is triune, and He is also triune in relation to time and to space.

Revelation 1:4 speaks of the first of the Trinity as He who is, and who was, and who is coming, or who is to come, or who is to be. The first of the Trinity must refer to the Father, and here the Father is called by such a divine title. Undoubtedly, such an expression is based upon the revelation of the Old Testament where Jehovah is referred to. This matter is fully revealed in Exodus chapter three (vv. 6, 14-16). There Jehovah, the great I Am, the great Eternal One, is the very God who is triune, the God of the father, Abraham, the God of the son, Isaac, and the God of the grandson, Jacob. Based upon Revelation 1:4 and Exodus 3, we can see that the Father God, as to His Person, is triune.

Second, the Father is triune in time because Revelation 1:4 says that He is the One who is, in the present, and who was, in the past, and who is coming, in the future. Therefore, we can see that the Father God is triune in relation to time.

Then the Father is also triune in space. You may have not considered this point before. Ephesians 4:6 tells us that God the Father is over all, through all, and in all. In relation to space, He is in three directions—above, through, and in. Therefore, we may say that the Father God is triune in relation to His Person, in relation to time, and in relation to space. This point has been more than clearly revealed in the holy Word, and we have seen it. To us this matter is a vision, not a doctrine.

CONCERNING THE SON

We have touched something of our vision concerning God and concerning the Father; now we come to our vision concerning the Son, Jesus Christ. Christ is the Triune God incarnated. We used to speak of the Son of God incarnated to be a man, but the Bible does not use such an expression.

The Entire God Incarnated

Strictly speaking, the Bible says, "In the beginning was the Word,...and the Word was God" (John 1:1). Here we need to realize that this God, whom the Word was, is not a partial God, not only God the Son, but God the Son, and God the Father, and God the Spirit, the entire God. The New Testament does not say the Word was God the Son; in fact, it does not say God the Son, nor God the Father, nor God the Spirit. The New Testament says that in the beginning was the Word, and the Word was the entire God, the Triune God, the Father, the Son, and the Spirit.

Furthermore, the Word became flesh (John 1:14). Therefore, Christ is the entire God, the Father, the Son, and the Spirit, incarnated. Strictly speaking, the New Testament does not say that the Word became a man, but it says that the Word became flesh. According to the New Testament usage, the flesh refers to the fallen man (Rom. 3:20). Nevertheless, it is with much hesitation that I say that Christ became a fallen man, lest you misunderstand and think that I am saying that Christ became a man with sin in Him. Certainly Christ did not become a man with sin in Him, but He did become a man after mankind had fallen. He became flesh only in the likeness of the flesh of sin (Rom. 8:3).

Apart from Sin but Joined to Sinful Humanity

There is a very strong note on John 1:14 in *The Ryrie Study Bible* (Moody Press, 1978, p. 1494) that boldly declares that Christ has joined Himself to sinful humanity: "Jesus Christ was unique, for He was God from all eternity and yet joined Himself to sinful humanity in the incarnation. The God-man possessed all the attributes of deity (Phil. 2:6) and the attributes common to humanity (apart from sin), and He will exist forever as the God-man in His resurrected body (Acts 1:11; Rev. 5:6). Only the God-man could be an adequate Savior; for He must be human in order to be able to suffer and die, and He must be God to make that death effective as a payment for sin." I have not found such a strong word on this matter in anyone else's notes, expositions, or commentaries. After his statement that Christ joined Himself to sinful humanity, Ryrie added the phrase "apart from sin."

It is crucial for us to see why the Bible does not say that Christ as the Triune God became a man. To say only that Christ became a man does not definitely denote that man was in a fallen condition at the time of the incarnation. However, according to the New Testament usage, to say that the Word became flesh definitely indicates that "the flesh" refers to the fallen man. Romans 3:20 confirms this: "By the works of law no flesh shall be justified before Him." At the time the Lord Jesus as the Triune God was incarnated to be a man, man had fallen already. Christ did not become a man before the fall, but He did so after the fall, while man was absolutely living in the fall. Therefore, as Ryrie says, He actually joined Himself to sinful humanity.

Nevertheless, we need to be very clear that there was no sin in the Lord's humanity. The fact that the Lord joined Himself to sinful humanity does not mean that there was sin in His humanity. There is no sin in Him, although He became flesh, which refers to the fallen man in whom is sin.

As the Brass Serpent, Having the Form of the Fallen Man but Not Having His Nature of Sin

In the same Gospel where it is recorded that the Triune God became the flesh (John 1:14), this Man Jesus, the Son of Man, told us, "As Moses lifted up the serpent in the wilderness, even so must the Son of Man be lifted up," that is, lifted up on the cross (3:14). This word indicates definitely that the incarnated Christ was portrayed in typology as a serpent, by the brass serpent in Numbers 21, a serpent in form but not in nature.

The brass serpent lifted up on the pole in Numbers 21

was a representative of the people bitten by the serpents (vv. 4-9). All the people who had been bitten by the serpents became serpents in the eyes of God. For God to forgive them, to save them, and to recover them, they needed to be judged by God. Nevertheless, they themselves were not judged, but they were judged in and through their representative, which was the serpent made of brass. In the eyes of God, that serpent lifted up on the pole and judged there was the representative of all those who had become serpents, but the brass serpent possessed only the form of the serpent and not the nature. Therefore, from the Gospel of John we can see that the incarnated One was in the form of a fallen man, but He did not have the fallen nature.

In the Likeness of the Flesh of Sin

In Romans 8:3 Paul tells us clearly that God sent His Son in the likeness of the flesh of sin. The major point in this verse is the flesh, but the flesh is limited by the word likeness, and the flesh is modified by the phrase "of sin." "In the likeness of the flesh of sin" is a wonderful phrase, a wonderful expression. On one hand, there is the flesh of sin, but on the other hand, there is only the likeness of the flesh of sin. These two modifiers indicate that the Triune God became the flesh as a fallen man only in the likeness of the flesh of sin, but not in the sinful nature. We need to be clear concerning this distinction.

Made Sin As One Who Knew No Sin

Moreover, our Christ in incarnation was made sin, although He knew no sin. Paul gives us an even stronger verse that corresponds to Romans 8:3 in 2 Corinthians 5:21: "Him who did not know sin He made sin on our behalf." Christ knew no sin, yet God made Him sin. To say that Christ was made sin is a much stronger expression than to say that He became flesh. Nevertheless, the Word clearly says that God made Him sin, and we need to be bold to declare what the Word declares. While Christ was being judged on the cross, in the eyes of God He was sin there. When we say that God made Christ sin, we have Paul's word in 2 Corinthians 5:21 as the Word of God to support us. Paul, however, adds a modifier, "Him who did not know sin." To say that God made One sin who knew no sin is to speak a heavenly language. How much we all need to learn to speak the heavenly language of the Bible!

Incarnated through the Mingling of Two Essences

Such a Christ who knew no sin, yet was made sin, was the very embodiment of the fullness of the Godhead of the Triune God when He lived on this earth in His incarnation. We may make such a statement based upon Colossians 2:9: "In Him dwells all the fullness of the Godhead bodily." Such a One was conceived and born of God with the divine essence mingled with the human essence. He was born of these two essences through the Holy Spirit and through the chaste virgin (Matt. 1:18-25; Luke 1:26-35; 2:1-7). Through the Holy Spirit He received the divine essence, and through the human virgin He received the human essence. The divine conception was a mingling. These two essences, the divine and the human, became mingled together in His divine conception.

Mingling means that two elements are joined and mingled together, but the two elements do not lose their particular natures. Their two natures retain their distinction, and they are not joined together to produce a third nature. Therefore, such a One was born to be a God-man who is both the complete God and the perfect man, possessing two natures and two lives, the divine nature and the divine life, and the human nature and the human life, mingled together as one but without any confusion, without any loss of their distinctive natures, and without anything produced to be a third nature or a third element. Such a short definition helps us to be clear about the incarnation of Christ and His Person in two natures with two kinds of life.

Passing through Human Living and an All-Inclusive Death

After He passed through conception and birth, such a wonderful Christ lived on this earth for more than thirty-three years. After fully tasting the human life, He entered into and passed through an all-inclusive death with a number of aspects.

As the Lamb of God

Firstly, Christ died as the Lamb of God to take away the sin (the totality of sin, including sins) of the world, that is, of mankind (John 1:29).

As a Man in the Flesh

Secondly, Christ died as a Man in the flesh causing sin to be condemned in the flesh by God (Rom. 8:3).

As the Last Adam

Thirdly, Christ died as the last Adam (1 Cor. 15:45b) Adam, the head of all mankind, made himself with all his descendants a fallen man in God's old creation through his fall. Christ, as the last Adam, as the conclusion of the old man, brought the old man to the cross to be crucified. When He was crucified our old man was crucified with Him (Rom. 6:6).

As a Creature

Fourthly, Christ died as a creature. Christ was the Firstborn, the first item, of all the old creation (Col. 1:15b). Christ as the first item of the old creation brought also the entire old creation to the cross to be terminated. This is based upon Colossians 1:20 where it says that all things were reconciled to God through Christ.

As a Serpent in Form

Fifthly, Christ died as a serpent in form (John 3:14) as

typified by the brass serpent in Numbers 21:9. In this aspect Christ died not only to be a substitute of the fallen men who had been bitten by the old serpent (Rev. 12:9), but also to destroy the old serpent, the Devil, who has the might of death (Heb. 2:14).

As the Peacemaker

Sixthly, Christ died on the cross also as the Peacemaker (Eph. 2:14-16). Due to man's fall, among mankind there are many ordinances, many customs, many habits, many different ways to live, and many different ways to worship. All these are the differences among peoples that have divided, scattered, and confused mankind. Therefore, among the human race there is no peace. Christ died on the cross as the Peacemaker to abolish all the ordinances to make God's chosen people and redeemed ones one new man.

As a Grain of Wheat

In addition, Christ died on the cross as a grain of wheat, sown into man's heart. This is the seventh aspect. As a grain of wheat, He died to release the divine life and to enliven God's redeemed ones, to produce many grains that can be blended together into a loaf to be offered to God. This loaf is the very church, the Body of Christ (1 Cor. 10:17).

All of us need to see such a vision. Christ died on the on the cross as at least seven items: as the Lamb of God, as a Man in the flesh, as the last Adam, as a creature, as a serpent in form, as the Peacemaker, and as a grain of wheat. On the negative side, He died to terminate all the negative things, and on the positive side, He died to release the divine life to produce the church. This is our vision.

Becoming the Life-giving Spirit and the Firstborn among Many Brothers

After such an all-inclusive death, Christ entered into

resurrection. In His resurrection He became a life-giving Spirit, who is the very consummation of the Triune God. The life-giving Spirit is the germinating Spirit because to give life is to germinate. Not only did Christ become the life-giving Spirit to impart life to all of His believers, but also in resurrection He became the firstborn Son of God to bring forth many sons of God to be His many brothers (Rom. 8:29). This is a crucial point in our vision concerning Christ.

CONCERNING THE SPIRIT

The Spirit of God and the Spirit of Jehovah

Concerning the Spirit, we have seen that He is the Spirit of God in God's creation (Gen. 1:2), and that He is also the Spirit of Jehovah in God's relationship with man (Judg. 3:10). In God's creation, He is the Spirit of God, and in God's relationship with man, He is the Spirit of Jehovah.

The Holy Spirit

In the initiation of God's New Testament economy, the Spirit is the Holy Spirit. The birth of John the Baptist and the birth of Jesus Christ are the initiation of God's New Testament economy. In this initiation, the Spirit is the Holy Spirit with whom the forerunner of God's New Testament economy, John the Baptist, was filled (Luke 1:15) and of whom the Savior, Jesus Christ, was conceived and born (Luke 1:35; Matt. 1:18, 20). Jesus was also anointed with this Holy Spirit to live and to minister to carry out a part of the New Testament ministry (Luke 3:22).

The Spirit

In the glorification (i.e. resurrection, Luke 24:26) of Jesus, the Spirit is "the Spirit" (John 7:39). We have seen that in God's creation, He is the Spirit of God; in God's relationship with man, He is the Spirit of Jehovah; in the initiation of the New Testament economy, He is the Holy Spirit; and in the glorification of Jesus, He is the Spirit. Here the Spirit is the consummation of the processed God who has passed through incarnation, human living, death and resurrection. From this point onward, He is called the Spirit of Jesus in Acts 16:7, the Spirit of Christ in Romans 8:9, the Spirit of Jesus Christ in Philippians 1:19, the Spirit of the Lord in 2 Corinthians 3:17, the Spirit of God in Romans 8:9, and the Spirit of life in Romans 8:2. The Spirit, after Jesus' glorification, became a compound Spirit as indicated by all these titles: the Spirit of God, the Spirit of the Lord, the Spirit of Jesus, the Spirit of Christ, the Spirit of Jesus Christ, and the Spirit of life. This all-inclusive, compound Spirit is compounded with Christ's deity, His humanity, His human life, His all-inclusive death and its effectiveness, His resurrection and its power, and His ascension and its exaltation, including the enthronement, the crowning with honor and glory, the headship, the lordship, and the kingship. Therefore, in this compound Spirit there are all the elements of Christ's divinity, humanity, human life, death with its effectiveness, resurrection with its power, and ascension with its exaltation. All these are the ingredients of this compound Spirit.

Therefore, the Spirit is the consummation of the processed Triune God, and He is all-inclusive. He is a compound of God, of man, of human living, of the all-inclusive, redeeming, terminating, and life-releasing death with its effectiveness, of the germinating resurrection with its power, and of the ascension with its exaltation. He is not only the consummation of the processed Triune God, but also the consummation of whatever the processed Triune God has achieved, attained, and obtained.

The Seven Spirits

In the book of Revelation, the Spirit becomes the seven Spirits (1:4; 3:1; 4:5; 5:6). The Spirit is not essentially seven. Essentially, He is only one, but economically, He is seven. Eventually, in God's economy and in His function, He becomes the sevenfold intensified Spirit. In essence, the Spirit is uniquely one, but in function, in economy, He is seven. In Revelation it is not a matter of the essence, but it is a matter of the function, of the economy. Economically speaking, the Spirit is intensified sevenfold. Without such a vision we cannot reconcile the two aspects, the Spirit being one and the Spirit being seven. However, with a clear vision concerning the difference between the Spirit essentially and the Spirit economically, the Lord has given us the way to reconcile the two sides of the truth.

CONCERNING GOD'S ECONOMY

We have covered the first four basic visions we have received of the Lord through these past sixty years, our vision concerning God, concerning the Father, concerning the Son, and concerning the Spirit. Now we come to our vision concerning God's economy.

God's Administration to Carry Out His Plan

In God's economy we have seen God's desire, which was in God's heart even before the foundation of the world. Second, we have also seen God's good pleasure. God has a desire and He has a good pleasure. Based on His pleasure, He made a plan; He formed a purpose with His plan and chose a number of people and predestinated them unto sonship. These are five crucial items: God's desire, His pleasure, His choice, His predestination, and His plan (Eph. 1:4-5, 9, 11; 3:11). For these five things God surely needs an economy, an arrangement, an administration, on a large scale. He needs a schedule to carry out His plan which is for His predestination, according to His choice, according to His pleasure, and according to His desire.

God's Dispensing of Himself into His Chosen People

The economy of God is to dispense Himself into His chosen, predestinated, and redeemed people as their life, their life supply, and their everything. We have spent much time to study the Greek word for economy or dispensation used in Ephesians 1:10; 3:9 and 1 Timothy

1:4—*oikonomia*. This Greek word is a compound word made up of *oikos*, meaning house, and *nomos*, meaning law. If you trace the root of this word, it goes back to a word that refers to the parceling out of food, the distributing of food as in parcels. This root word also means to distribute food to the cattle for grazing. It is God's economy to parcel Himself out to us as our life and as our life supply.

In God's economy He dispenses Himself into His people as life, as life supply, and as everything to them. He dispenses Himself as their strength, their power, their wisdom, their righteousness, their holiness, their love, their kindness, and even as their attributes and virtues. This is God's economy. Out of this economy many believers are being produced to be the components of the Body of God's Son for a full expression of the Triune God. This is our vision concerning God's economy.

THE URGENT NEED TODAY

Brothers, I surely hope you all could spend time to get into these five matters concerning our vision of God, of the Father, of Christ, of the Spirit, and of God's economy. Every point is fully and properly grounded in particular verses of the Bible, which you can find with the help of the Life-studies.

If I can speak concerning all these things without any notes and pass on all these points to you, surely all of you who are younger than I am can get into these matters until you can speak spontaneously of our vision concerning God, the Father, the Son, the Spirit, and God's economy. I would strongly encourage all of you to get into these matters. If you do, wherever you go, you will speak concerning these things in a way that will stir up the interest of everyone you meet. There is no need to make your topic interesting. Your speaking along these lines will stir up the interest of others, and there will be no end to their interest. These points are exhaustless, and every one of them needs a lot of definition. The more you speak along these lines, the more you increase the interest of others, and the more you increase their appetite, their thirst, and their hunger. What we need is for all of us to see God's New Testament ministry and to see the vision in the Lord's recovery today. Surely we would not go back to pick up all of the old things that cannot meet today's need. The Lord's recovery has received a particular vision that is based upon the divine revelation concerning His New Testament ministry. I would encourage you all to spend adequate time to get into this vision in a full way.

CHAPTER TWO

THE VISION CONCERNING REDEMPTION AND CONCERNING GOD'S FULL SALVATION

To have a clear understanding concerning the Triune God, concerning redemption, and concerning God's full salvation according to the revelation of the pure Word of God is not a simple matter for us today. The hardship is always due to the traditional teaching we have received in the past concerning these matters. The teachings we have received in a traditional way have become a frustration to our vision.

CONCERNING REDEMPTION

The Accomplisher

To know Christ's redemption we first need to know the Accomplisher of this redemption. If we know the Accomplisher, the Redeemer, then we surely know His redemption. We need to realize who Christ was at the very time He was condemned and put to death to suffer God's just and righteous judgment. This matter needs to be considered very carefully because it involves the so-called theology concerning the Trinity and concerning Christology, the study of the Person of Christ. Our Redeemer, dying there to accomplish redemption for us, was the Head of all creation, the Firstborn of all creation, and also the image of the invisible God.

The Firstborn of All Creation

For Christ to be the Head of all creation involves the

matter of Christ being the Firstborn of all creation. In Colossians 1:15, speaking of Christ as a portion allotted to us by God, Paul tells us firstly that Christ is the image of the invisible God, and also that He is the Firstborn of all creation. In Colossians 1:15 we see, on the one hand, that Christ is related to God. He is the image of the invisible God, the expression of God, or the invisible God expressed.

On the other hand, Christ is related to all of the creation, and He is the Firstborn of all creation. For Christ to be the Firstborn of all creation means that He is the first item of all the creatures. Due to the heresy of Arius, not many Bible teachers would take this point in Colossians 1:15 according to the literal meaning of the Greek. Arius taught that Christ was not divine, that He was not God, but was rather something created by God in eternity, and he based his heretical teaching on Colossians 1:15. According to history, Arius was condemned because of his heresy and cast out, even exiled, by the Nicene Council in A.D. 325. Due to this heretical teaching of Arius, from the time of the Nicene Council until today, most of the Bible teachers would not interpret Colossians 1:15 according to the literal translation, for fear that they might be condemned for heresy as Arius was.

We have studied this phrase, "the Firstborn of all creation," carefully according to the Greek, and we have the assurance that this is an absolutely accurate translation. Some translators have even changed the translation to "the Firstborn before all creation." Every Greek student, no need to say the Greek scholars, can recognize that this kind of translation is altogether inaccurate. To change the preposition from "of" to "before" would indicate that Christ is something apart from the creatures, but to use the preposition "of" indicates that Christ is one of the creatures. There is a big difference. The reason some teachers would change the translation is that they are afraid of being condemned if they say that Christ is one of the creatures, even the first one of the creatures. Therefore, they dare not say that Christ is the Firstborn of all creation.

Some teachers have even interpreted Christ being the Firstborn of all creation to mean merely that Christ was prior to all creation. They say that He was the Creator and that He could never be a creature. They avoid saying that Christ is one of the creatures.

One expositor says that according to the Greek this phrase must be translated "the Firstborn of all creation," and he says that the word "of" as a preposition in Greek indicates that the Firstborn is one of the many items of the creatures. Even though he admits that this is the meaning according to the Greek, he goes on to say that we must avoid saying that Christ is one of the creatures. His own word is contradictory. He did not have the courage to interpret this verse according to the literal meaning.

The Creator and the Creature

Since 1958 I have put out some writings to declare that our Christ is surely not only the Creator but also a creature because He is both God, as the Creator, and man, as a creature. If you say that Christ is God, surely He is the Creator. If you say that He is a man, surely He is a creature. The strange thing is this: Although a good number of Christian teachers admit that Christ is a man, they do not have the courage to admit that He is a creature. How could it be that there is a man who is not a creature? Such an interpretation is illogical, yet many teachers dare not say that Christ is a creature.

To deny that Christ is a creature is to fall into an error in the line of the heresy of the Docetists (A. D. 70-170). The Docetists followed Gnosticism to say that all matter is evil, that every physical thing, including our flesh, is evil. The Docetists taught that Christ is holy and therefore He could never become matter, He could never become a physical thing, He could never become the flesh. Their heretical teaching was that Christ was not a genuine man, but that as a man He was merely a phantom. The teaching of Docetism was heresy.

Those who deny the truth that Christ as a man is a creature unknowingly make themselves Docetists, which is equal to saying that they do not confess that Christ has come in the flesh. John condemned such ones in chapter four of his first Epistle.

Christ is a man, a typical man with flesh, skin, bone, and blood. If you count these four items, you must admit that skin is something created, and that bone, flesh, and blood are all something of the creatures. It would be ridiculous to say that Christ is a man but that He is not a creature. This is not a matter of doctrinal debate. We need to take care of the truth, and we need to know the facts.

The Redeemer of Creation and Mankind

The redemption accomplished by Christ is not only for man but also for all creation. Chapter one of Colossians first tells us that Christ is the Firstborn of all creation (v. 15) and then that through Christ's redemption all the created things in heaven and on earth are reconciled to God (v. 20). Christ's redemption is for all things. Hebrews 2:9 says clearly that Christ tasted death not only on behalf of every man but also on behalf of everything.

If Christ were only a man and not the Firstborn of all creation, the first item of all the creatures, how could He accomplish redemption for all the creatures? In the same way that it is necessary for Him to be a man to accomplish redemption for man, it is necessary for Him to be a creature to make a redemption for all the creatures. It is necessary for our Redeemer to be the first item of all creation in order for Him to redeem all creation; therefore, He is in the first place as the Firstborn of all creation. In the same principle, He is the last Adam, the head of all mankind, and as such He is qualified to be the Redeemer of mankind.

Jesus, the Son of God

As the Firstborn of all creation, Christ is qualified to be the Redeemer of all creation, and as the last Adam of all mankind, He is qualified to be the Redeemer of mankind. However, if He were only the first item of all creatures and the last Adam of mankind, although He is altogether qualified to be the Redeemer, His redemption could not be eternally effective. If He were only one item of the creatures, how could one item die for all the creatures? If He were only a man, how could one man die for all men? In that case, the effectiveness of His redemption could not be eternal and lasting. If Christ's redemption were only a redemption accomplished by the first item of all the creatures and by the last Adam of mankind, His redemption would not be eternally and everlastingly effective. Such a redemption could never be eternal because neither a creature nor a man is eternal. It is necessary for our Redeemer to have some further qualification. There must be some element that is eternal, and that element must be God Himself. It is necessary for our Redeemer to be the very God.

When our Redeemer died on the cross, He died there as the first item of all the creation, as the last Adam, that is, as the head of all mankind, and as the very God. Because He died there as these three, His redemption is called the eternal redemption (Heb. 9:12). The first two aspects qualified Him to be the Redeemer, and the last aspect insures that His redemption is eternal, that it can cover everything, and also that it would be everlasting. For this reason, Christ is qualified to accomplish a redemption that is adequate and eternal.

When John told us that the blood that cleanses us, or that redeems us, is the blood of Jesus, he added the title, "His Son," the Son of God (1 John 1:7). The blood shed on the cross is the blood not only of the man Jesus, but also of Jesus the Son of God. The blood of Jesus is the genuine blood of a man. Only man's blood can redeem man. Of course, God does not have blood to shed, but even if He did have blood that He could shed, that blood would not be qualified to redeem man. Man should be redeemed by man's blood. Therefore, the blood of Jesus is the genuine blood of a genuine man which is altogether qualified to redeem man.

Nevertheless, if the blood of Jesus is only the blood of a man, it has nothing to insure its eternal effectiveness. Therefore, in 1 John 1:7 the Apostle John adds the title, His Son, the Son of God, to indicate His divinity. This Jesus is not only the Son of Man to shed the blood of a genuine man, but He is also the Son of God to insure the effectiveness of His blood for eternity.

The name Jesus denotes the Lord's humanity, which is needed for the shedding of the redeeming blood, and the title His Son denotes the Lord's divinity, which is needed for the eternal efficacy of the redeeming blood. Therefore, the blood of Jesus His Son indicates that this blood is the proper blood of a genuine man for redeeming God's fallen creatures with divine surety for its eternal efficacy, an efficacy which is all-prevailing in space and everlasting in time.

Therefore, our Redeemer was the first item of all the creatures, the last Adam of mankind, and the very God Himself. This truth involves a number of points which cause debate in theology. However, we do not care for debate; we care for the truth.

The God-Man with the Human and Divine Essences As His Constituents

We need to see the essences, the constituents, of the being of this One who was crucified on the cross and whose name was Jesus Christ. We know that He was crucified on the cross as One constituted of the human and divine essences because He had been conceived and born of these two essences. He was conceived of the Holy Spirit and born of a human virgin, with the divine essence mingled with the human essence. He is not merely human, but He is essentially both human and divine because He has been constituted with these two essences. These two essences are His constitution, His intrinsic Being.

When the Lord Jesus was baptized, He was baptized as One who possessed the divine essence and the human essence. All the others who were baptized were baptized as those who only possessed the human essence. There was only One by the name of Jesus who was baptized with two essences.

After His baptism, the Holy Spirit came down and descended upon the Lord Jesus. Based upon this fact, Cerinthus taught his great heresy that Jesus Himself did not have the Holy Spirit, but He was only human. (See footnote 22[1] in 1 John 2, *Recovery Version*.) Cerinthus in his heresy separated the earthly man Jesus from the Christ who is divine. He taught that the Holy Dove was a sign of the Christ who is divine, and that Christ as the Holy Dove, the Holy Spirit, descended upon the man Jesus after His baptism. He taught that this Christ as the divine Dove was with Jesus from that time for three and a half years, and that the divine Dove left Jesus when He went to the cross and was crucified. In other words, in his heresy Cerinthus taught that Christ left Jesus.

Cerinthus might have used two verses as a base for this part of his heresy. First, Matthew 3:16 says that the Holy Dove descended upon Jesus after His baptism. It might have been based upon this fact that Cerinthus taught that Jesus had nothing divine before the descending of the Holy Dove. Then, when Jesus was crucified on the cross, at the beginning of the last three hours at noon, He cried out, "My God, My God, why have You forsaken Me?" (Matt. 27:46). It might have been based upon this verse that Cerinthus taught that the Holy Dove went away and left only the man Jesus on the cross.

It may seem that Cerinthus could be right on this point, that he could have some ground for his interpretation of these verses. However, we need to look into this matter further. According to the cry of the Lord Jesus Himself, it is true that God left Jesus on the cross for man's sin. But we need to consider who was left on the cross. Was He merely a man of human essence? We need to see clearly that the One who was left on the cross was the same One already constituted of the human essence and the divine essence before His baptism. Before He was baptized and the Holy Spirit descended upon Him, this One was divine already, constituted with the divine essence. This is a crucial point. Therefore, it was not merely a man who was baptized, but a God-man who was baptized. In the same principle, it was not merely a man who was crucified, but a God-man who was crucified.

Therefore, in our Redeemer, while He was crucified on the cross for us sinners, there was the human essence—He was a man as the first creature and as the last Adam, the head of all mankind. In this Redeemer there was also the divine essence, because He is also God. With His human essence He was the first item of the creatures and the last Adam of mankind. With His divine essence He was God. God's leaving Christ on the cross is another aspect. This is the same as the time that the Holy Spirit descended upon Him when He was standing there after His baptism. For the Holy Spirit to descend upon Him did not indicate that He did not yet have the divine essence, because He had been constituted of it already. He was conceived with the divine essence and born of the divine essence before the time of His baptism. In the same principle, for God to depart from Christ on the cross did not indicate that He was no longer constituted with the divine essence. These points may seem to be quite complicated, but I hope they could be made clear to all of you.

The Sequence of the Trinity

At this juncture we need to go back to consider a further point concerning the sequence of the Trinity. In the Trinity we have seen the Father, we have seen the Son, Christ, and we have seen the Spirit. It is correct to say that in the Trinity the First is the Father, the Second is the Son, and the Third is the Spirit. However, we need to see that the sequence of the Trinity is changed when it comes to the matter of the application to us.

Not only in Revelation 1 does the Third become the Second (vv. 4-5), but the same principle has been applied elsewhere. In Ephesians 3 Paul says that he prays to the Father that He may strengthen you through His Spirit (here the Spirit is mentioned second) that Christ may make His home in your heart. In such an application, the Third becomes the Second, which is in principle the same as in Revelation 1. Furthermore, 1 Peter 1:2 indicates that we were chosen by the Father through the sanctification of the Spirit according to the blood of Christ. Here again the Spirit is ranked as the Second. In addition, the sequence of the Trinity is also changed in 2 Corinthians 13:14 where Paul speaks of the grace of the Lord Jesus Christ, the love of God, and the fellowship of the Holy Spirit. In this case, the sequence is changed in the application to us with the Second (Christ) becoming the First, and the First becoming the Second.

These changes in the sequence in the Trinity indicate that function is one thing, and essence is another. In function the Trinity is mentioned in a sequence that is different from His sequence in essence. In addition, as we have seen in the matter of the seven Spirits, the Spirit is essentially one, but economically seven. Because some early teachers discovered this principle, they invented terms such as the essential Trinity and the economical Trinity.

The Essential and Economical Trinity
in Christ's Redemption

In the essential Trinity, the Three are all there without anything that we might call a succession or a progression. The Father, the Son, and the Spirit were all there at the same time in eternity, and They are here; They continue to exist simultaneously for eternity. This is in the essential Trinity, the divine Trinity according to His essence.

However, in the economical Trinity, initially, the Father planned, He made His choice, His selection, and He predestinated. Following this planning of the Father, the Son came to accomplish what the Father had planned. Then, after the Son's accomplishment, the Spirit came to apply what the Son had accomplished according to what the Father had planned. Here in this economy there is a succession, and there is a progression. Therefore, according to the essence of the Trinity, the Three are equal, and there is no succession or progression. Nevertheless, in the economy of God, there is what we might call a succession, a progression. There are the three steps.

We need to realize that Christ's redemption involves both God's essence and God's economy. For the Redeemer to be qualified He needs two essences—the essence of man and the essence of God. However, when He accomplished redemption, economically speaking, there were some matters regarding the functioning Spirit. While the Redeemer was standing there after His baptism, the Holy Spirit came down upon Him economically. That descending of the Spirit was the functioning Spirit, the Spirit in function, or the Spirit in God's economy. However, when He was conceived and born of the Holy Spirit, the Holy Spirit there was the Holy Spirit in essence. These distinctions are important for our understanding, but they may not be easy for us to grasp.

When the Redeemer was crucified on the cross, God left Him, not essentially, but economically. God was essentially in the man Jesus from His conception, through His birth, through His human living, through His death, through His resurrection, and through eternity. However, after He was baptized to begin to minister, God came down upon Him to anoint Him economically. This economical Spirit was with Him all the time for three and a half years. Then, according to Hebrews 9:14, He offered Himself to God through the eternal Spirit. At the last period of time on the cross, when He became sin in the eyes of God, this Spirit left Him economically, not essentially. This means that God left Him economically, not essentially. It is by this way, essentially and economically, that He was qualified to redeem man and all creatures and also entitled to have the eternal efficacy for His redemption. Therefore, He is qualified to accomplish our redemption, and the eternal and everlasting effectiveness of His redemption is insured. This is our vision concerning Christ's redemption.

At this point, may I say a brief word concerning the reason we have no trust in the traditional teachings. We have a vision with much deeper truth. Because the Lord has shown us something in a much deeper way, we simply cannot follow the teachings that are superficial.

CONCERNING GOD'S FULL SALVATION

It is not easy to speak concerning our vision of redemption, nor is it easy to speak concerning the vision of God's salvation. However, once you are enlightened to see this vision, you would be beside yourself. Compared to the full salvation revealed in the Word of God, our speaking may be somewhat like the speaking of an uneducated person about a highly technical subject if we are short of enlightenment and short of vision in this matter.

The Assurance of Salvation

In the first stage of our vision concerning God's full salvation, we were enlightened to see the assurance of salvation. We were beside ourselves. Wherever we went, we would ask people, "Have you been saved? Do you know that you have been saved?" We especially liked to ask the pastors, elders, preachers, deacons, or deaconesses these questions. At that time I was somewhat like a young tiger, afraid of nothing and not knowing much. We offended many people. I was a young man, about twenty-five years old, and I was questioning a pastor about sixty-five years old, "Do you know you have been saved?" No doubt he was offended and wondered how such a young person dared to ask him such a question. Actually, he did not know that he was saved. We met a number of cases like this.

On one occasion in 1933, I was invited to preach to the students at a Presbyterian Hospital nursing school with nearly one hundred students and nurses. The pastor, the only older one present, sat at the back of the chapel behind all the students, while I was standing in the front preaching the assurance of salvation. He was offended quite a few times while I was speaking and shook his head in disagreement. The students, however, were happy to hear what I had to say, and they nodded their heads in agreement. As I said, at that time I was young and very bold, but I did not know much. Today, if I were preaching the assurance of salvation, I would not ask people, "Have you been saved?" In fact, if you were to ask me whether I have been saved, today I would ask you what you mean, because I have come to realize that God's salvation is not a simple matter.

The Stages of God's Salvation

Because God's salvation is not a simple matter or a matter that can be summarized in a brief way, it is necessary to explain what we mean when we speak of being saved. There are a number of stages involved in God's full salvation.

For example, in chapter one of Philippians Paul said that he was in prison, and he indicated that the prayer of the saints and the bountiful supply of the Spirit of Jesus Christ would be salvation unto him (v. 19). This meant that Paul had not been saved yet, but that he would be saved by the saints' prayer and the bountiful supply of the Spirit of Jesus Christ. Therefore, we can see that it is necessary to explain specifically what we mean when we ask, "Have you been saved?" We need to understand the stages of God's salvation in full.

I would like to ask each of you whether or not you have been saved, and then I would ask whether you have been saved from the unhappy expression on your wife's face, and whether you have been saved from all your worries. Therefore, we would say again that God's salvation is not a simple matter, and it is a salvation in stages. To be saved from God's condemnation is one thing, but to be saved from Satan's usurpation is something else. To be saved from environmental botherings is another matter, and to be saved from God's punishment, from His discipline, is still another matter.

Furthermore, man has three parts, and every part has become fallen. As a tripartite man with a spirit, soul, and body, you need to be saved in every part. Your body needs to be saved out of its fallen condition. Your soul and your spirit likewise need to be saved out of the fall. The two things the fall mainly brought to you are sin and death. Therefore, to be saved you need to be saved from sin, and you need to be saved from death.

How many items we need to be saved from! You need to consider all the things you need to be saved from. You need to be saved from God's condemnation, which includes saving us from hell, or from the lake of fire; you need to be saved from Satan's usurpation; and you need to be saved from environmental troubles. You also need to be saved from God's punishment, His discipline. You need to have your body saved from sin and death, you need to have your soul saved from corruption and death, and you need your spirit saved from death. Even with such a list of items, there are many more things involved in God's salvation that we have not mentioned yet. God's salvation is full and all-inclusive. When you try to explain what we have seen of God's full salvation, it is necessary for you to cover all of the aforementioned points.

Compositional Salvation

God's salvation is a compositional matter for the

salvation of our spirit, our soul, and our body. It is composed with the forgiveness and washing away of sins, then with justification, reconciliation, redemption, regeneration, sanctification, transformation, transfiguration, conformation, and glorification. These items composed together equal salvation. Such a compositional salvation saves us from God's condemnation and from so many negative things.

First this compositional salvation saves your spirit. To save your spirit is the initial stage of God's saving by regeneration. Then from this initial stage, God's compositional salvation goes on to save your soul by sanctification and transformation. Then this compositional salvation goes on to save your body by transfiguration, including conformation and glorification, which makes you no longer different from the Lord. It is necessary to cover all these points to have the vision of God's full salvation.

CHAPTER THREE

THE VISION CONCERNING THE BELIEVERS AND CONCERNING THE CHURCH

CONCERNING THE BELIEVERS

The vision concerning the believers is very crucial, central, and dynamic in the Lord's recovery. The believers are those who were fallen sinners and who have been saved by the grace of God (Eph. 2:8) through their God-given and God-allotted faith (2 Pet. 1:1), which has brought them into an organic union with the Triune God in Christ (1 Cor. 6:17). Such an organic union with the Triune God is to be in union with Christ in His death, His resurrection, and His ascension, since the Triune God has passed through Christ's death, resurrection, and ascension. When we are in union with Christ, we are in union with the processed God.

These believers have been forgiven of their sins (Acts 10:43), which have been washed away by the redeeming blood of Christ (1 John 1:7). They have been justified by God in Christ (Acts 13:39; 1 Cor. 6:11), and they have been reconciled to God (Rom. 5:10), so they have been redeemed back to God (Rev. 5:9). Based upon this, they have been regenerated in their spirit by the Spirit of God (John 3:6) to be the children of God unto the divine sonship (John 1:12-13; Rom. 8:16) and to be the members of Christ (Eph. 5:30) unto His stature (Eph. 4:13) to be His fullness (Eph. 1:23).

These believers possess the divine life (1 John 5:11-13) and partake of the divine nature (2 Pet. 1:4) in addition to their human life and human nature. They are joined in their spirit to the Lord (1 Cor. 6:17) who is the Spirit. Thus, they are one spirit with the Lord, and such a spirit is a mingled spirit. The believers should constantly live a life in union with the Triune God in such a mingled spirit.

The Issues of Being One Spirit with the Lord

The believers' being one spirit with the Lord issues in four things. First, they should walk according to the mingled spirit by the law of the Spirit of life that they might be freed from the law of sin and of death (Rom. 8:2). Second, due to their union with Christ in His death, resurrection, and ascension, Christ lives in them (Gal. 2:20), and Christ is to be formed in them (Gal. 4:19) that they may live Christ and magnify Christ (Phil. 1:20-21). Third, they should be transformed in their soul by the renewing of its parts (Rom. 12:2), the mind, the emotion, and the will, into the image of Christ from glory to glory (2 Cor. 3:18) that they may mature in the growth of life (1 Cor. 3:6-7). Finally, they should be built up in the Body of Christ by the growth in life unto the full measure of the stature of Christ (Eph. 4:13-16). These issues of the believers' being one spirit with the Lord are brief yet all-inclusive.

At the Lord's Coming

During the Lord's tarrying to come back, many of the believers died. Many of these died without maturity in life, and they died in the way of being defeated. After all the believers die, they go to Paradise (Luke 23:43), a pleasant section, a section of comfort, in Hades where the dead are kept (Luke 16:22-23, 25-26). Then the living believers will remain until the Lord's coming back, which is His *parousia*, a Greek word meaning presence (see note 3[3] in Matthew 24—Recovery Version). At the Lord's *parousia* the living believers will be raptured according to maturity. Those who mature first will be raptured first (Rev. 14:1-4). At the last rapture of the saints, all the dead ones will be resurrected and raptured with all the living saints to the air (1 Thes. 4:15-17). At this point, all the believers, dead or living, will appear before the judgment seat of Christ to be judged concerning their way of living after they have been regenerated (2 Cor. 5:10). The faithful ones will be rewarded (Matt. 25:21) to inherit the kingdom of God and of Christ in the millenium for them to share Christ's joy and kingship for one thousand years (Matt. 25:21, 23; Rev. 20:6). The unfaithful believers will be assigned with a dispensational discipline (1 Cor. 3:15; Luke 12:47-48). This discipline will be a type of punishment during the millennium for them to become matured in life.

The Dispensation of the Kingdom—
A Time for God to Perfect His Redeemed People

This coming kingdom is used by the Lord as an incentive to encourage the believers in this age to live Him in a victorious way, as a reward to the faithful ones, and as a way to cause immature believers to mature so they will be fully perfected to enter into the new heaven and new earth to participate in the eternal life in the New Jerusalem. This means that the millenium, the last one thousand years of the old creation, will be a dispensation for God to perfect His chosen, predestinated, called, and redeemed believers. Some Christian teachers think that the thousand years of the millenium as a dispensation is not for God's perfecting of His redeemed people. They think that God's perfection of His redeemed people will end with the present dispensation of grace. However, according to the vision we have seen, the coming one thousand years will still be a period of time in the old creation. As long as the time is still in the old creation, it will still be time for God to perfect His redeemed people. This means God will have used four dispensations, the dispensation before law, the dispensation of law, the dispensation of grace, and the dispensation of the kingdom, to perfect all His chosen and redeemed people.

He perfected some in the first dispensation before law, such as Abel, Enos, Enoch, Noah, Abraham, Isaac, Jacob, and Joseph. These patriarchs were fully perfected by God during the first dispensation. Now they are in Paradise waiting for the time to come when they will share the eternal blessing of the eternal life in the dispensation of the kingdom and consummately in the New Jerusalem. God also used the second dispensation, the dispensation of law, to prepare people like Moses, Joshua, and Caleb. Hebrews 11 gives us a list of the names of some saints whom God perfected in the first two dispensations. Then God used the third dispensation, the dispensation of grace, to perfect thousands of faithful believers, including Peter, James, John, Paul, Stephen, the other apostles, and all the faithful ones throughout the centuries until the present day. We must realize, though, that a good number of God's chosen ones were not perfected in the first dispensation before law. Many of God's chosen ones were not perfected, yet they were chosen. Many were not perfected in the second dispensation of law. Also, in the third dispensation, the dispensation of grace, a great many believers who were genuinely chosen by God never were matured in life before they died. They were not perfected. Surely God would not give up all of these unperfected believers who had been chosen and predestinated by Him in eternity. Romans 11:29 tells us that "the free gifts and the calling of God are irrevocable." Therefore, God will use the last dispensation, the dispensation of the kingdom, to discipline these unfaithful ones in the preceding dispensations to cause them to grow in life unto maturity that they might be fully perfected for the coming eternal blessing of eternal life in the New Jerusalem. After God's continual perfecting work throughout the four dispensations, all of God's chosen, predestinated, and redeemed ones will be fully perfected. Then the old creation will be over and the new universe will come in where all of these fully perfected, God-chosen ones will be transferred into the new heaven and new earth to enjoy the New Jerusalem as their eternal blessing of the eternal life. This is a sketch of the vision the Lord has shown us in His recovery concerning the believers.

CONCERNING THE CHURCH

A Mystery

The church is a mystery (Eph. 3:4; 5:32). This mystery was in the Triune God, in the Father, in the Son, and in the Spirit. With the believers there is also an amount of mystery, but not as much as with the church. The mystery of God in Colossians 2:2 is Christ; whereas the mystery of Christ in Ephesians 3:4 is the church. God is a mystery, and Christ, as the embodiment of God to express Him, is the mystery of God. Christ is also a mystery, and the church, as the Body of Christ to express Him, is the mystery of Christ. The divine mystery is much more with the church corporately than with the saints individually. The church is a corporate unit which is produced out of Christ who is the mystery of God. This all-inclusive Christ is a mystery of the mysterious God and such a Christ as the mystery of God produces a unit which is the church. By this we can realize that the church is the continuation of the mystery which is Christ. Mystery surely produces mystery. Whatever you are, you bring forth. Christ, who is the mystery of God, brings forth the church, the mystery of Christ.

To see and to understand such a mystery our human mentality is altogether inadequate. This is why the apostle Paul prayed that God would give us a spirit of wisdom and revelation (Eph. 1:17) that we may understand the church which is the mystery of Christ.

A Pure Product out of Christ

The church is nothing more than a pure product out of Christ. This is typified by Eve in the book of Genesis. Eve was fully, completely, and purely produced out of Adam

(Gen. 2:21-24). Within Eve there was nothing else but Adam. Beside the Adamic element, there was no other element in Eve. Whatever was in Eve and whatever Eve was was Adam. Eve was a full reproduction of Adam. Adam and Eve are a type of Christ and the church (Eph. 5:30-32; Gen. 2:22-24). The church must also be one element—the element of Christ. Other than Christ's element there should be no other element in the church. Such a vision will cause us to mourn over today's situation. Within Christianity today there is very little of the element of Christ. Instead, innumerable elements other than Christ can be seen. In the Lord's recovery, however, the church must be the pure element of Christ. Anything that is other than Christ is not the church.

"Christly," "Resurrectionly," and Heavenly

After Christ terminated the entire old creation through His all-inclusive death, the church was produced in His resurrection (1 Pet. 1:3; Eph. 2:6). The church is an entity absolutely in resurrection; it is not natural, nor is it of the old creation. The church is a new creation created in Christ's resurrection and by the resurrected Christ. We must see this vision. In addition to seeing that the church was produced in Christ's resurrection, we must also see where the church is. The church today is in Christ in ascension. Ephesians 2:6 tells us that the church has been resurrected with Christ, and now the church is seated in the heavenlies with Christ. Therefore, the church is absolutely and purely of the element of Christ, absolutely in resurrection, and absolutely remaining in the heavenlies with Christ. The English language does not give us adequate adjective forms for the nouns Christ and resurrection. We must, therefore, invent some new vocabulary words to communicate such a vision of the church. We may say that today the church is "Christly," "resurrectionly," and heavenly. These three adjectives describe the fact conveyed in the Bible. The church is of Christ; the church is of resurrection; the church is of the heavens. The church is Christly, resurrectionly, and heavenly. With the church there is no element other than Christ. Such a vision will govern you to the uttermost and will rule out everything that is not Christly (of Christ), resurrectionly (of resurrection), or heavenly (of the heavens). With the believers there is still the flesh of sin, but with the church there is no flesh of sin because the church was born in resurrection (1 Pet. 1:3). The church is a matter in Christ, in resurrection, and in Christ's ascension in the heavenlies.

The Outward Aspect of the Church

The church, outwardly speaking, is a congregation called out of the world unto God for God's purpose. The Greek word for the church is *ekklesia* which means a called out congregation, a meeting, a gathering, or an assembly, called out for a purpose (Matt. 16:18; 18:17). It is much better to translate this word *ekklesia* into assembly. The Brethren teachers insisted on translating *ekklesia* in this way, so they were known as the Brethren assemblies. The church is God's *ekklesia,* which is composed of all the believers as a congregation called out of the world by God for His purpose. This is why we must gather together. We must assemble and meet in order to have a congregation, a composition, for God to work and to move among us. This is the outward aspect of the church.

The Inward Essence of the Church and its Function

We must also see the inward essence of the church. Without the inward aspect, the church is a mere organization. The church, however, should be an organism. We believers are not only composed together, but we are organically united together. As a result, we are not an organization but an organic composition which is an organism. We are not merely together, but we are growing together. We do not grow together separately like the trees in a forest, but we grow together organically like the members of a person's physical body. A particular member of a person's body organically grows together with all the other members. In like manner, we, as members of the Body of Christ (Eph. 5:30), are growing with the growth of God (Col. 2:19).

It is essential that we go further to see the inward essence of the church and its function. First, the church is the house of God (1 Tim. 3:15; Eph. 2:19; 1 Pet. 2:5), God's dwelling place, God's temple, which is in Christ, in resurrection, and in the heavenlies. The church is also the Body of Christ (Eph. 1:22-23a) because Christ Himself is God's temple, God's dwelling, God's house (John 2:19-22). To be the Body of Christ is to be God's dwelling, God's house, God's temple. Jesus told the Jews in John 2:19: "Destroy this temple, and in three days I will raise it up." In this verse the Lord was speaking of the temple of His Body (v. 21). In resurrection, this temple has been enlarged (1 Pet. 1:3; 1 Cor. 3:16-17). Now the house of God is in its expansion. God's dwelling expanded is Christ with His Body (Eph. 2:19-22; 1 Cor. 3:16). This Body is in Christ, in resurrection, and in the heavenlies so this Body is the composition, the constitution, of all the unsearchable riches of Christ (Eph. 3:8). Such a constitution, such a composition, becomes the fullness, the expression, of the One who fills all in all (Eph. 1:23b). The church is also the new man, which is corporate and universal (Eph. 2:15). There are many believers, but there is only one new man in the universe. All the believers are components of this one corporate and universal new man.

This one in function is Christ's Body, and in love, in satisfaction, this one is Christ's counterpart, His wife (Eph. 5:25, 29, 32). His Body is for His expression. His wife is for His satisfaction. This church is also a warrior, fighting with Christ against God's enemy to destroy him (Eph. 6:10-17). According to the vision we have seen concerning the church, the last aspect of the church in this age is the lampstand which is the very embodiment of the

Triune God (Rev. 1:12-13, 20). The house, the Body, the fullness, the wife, and the warrior eventually are the very embodiment of the Triune God. The lampstand embodies the Triune God in His divine essence, in His divine shape, and for His divine expression.

When the church arrives at the state of being the very embodiment of the Triune God, the church will be ready for the marriage of the Lamb (Rev. 19:7); this is the readiness of the bride for the bridegroom to come to marry her (John 3:29). This wife will be a composition of all the faithful, overcoming, matured believers who will inherit the kingdom of God and Christ in the millennium to share Christ's joy and feast with Him for a thousand years (Rev. 19:7-9). These ones will be the wife of Christ in the millennium and will not include the defeated ones, the unfaithful ones, since the unfaithful ones still will not be matured during the millennium. Their maturity will be built up during the millennium. After being dealt with by the Lord during the millennium, they will participate in the New Jerusalem for eternity. After the millennium, in the new heaven and the new earth, this church who is the wife of the Lamb in the one thousand years of the millennium, will consummate in the New Jerusalem. The New Jerusalem will be the consummation of the church which includes all the Old Testament saints. This is a vision concerning the church in its essence and in its functions.

The Practicality of the Church

In its practice the church exists in different localities on this earth during this age, so the universal church in its practicality becomes local. In its universal nature it is one, but in its local practice it is many. There is one universal church in essence, but there are many local churches in practice. In any locality there should only be one church (Rev. 1:11). In its universal aspect (Matt. 16:18) the church is composed of all the believers in all places at all times (1 Cor. 12:13). In its local aspect (Matt. 18:17) the church is composed of the believers in one locality at one time (Phil. 1:1; Acts 8:1; 13:1; Rom. 16:1). Anything more than one church in one locality is not proper.

Being Governed by this Vision

We must see the church in its essence, its function, and its practicality. This vision will govern us and rule out all other elements. Any natural, fleshly, or ambitious element will be ruled out by this vision. Under this vision we do not have the boldness to exercise anything of our natural man. In this respect, such a vision paralyzes us. Most Christians realize that the church is a constitution, a composition, of all the believers in Christ. By the Lord's mercy, however, what we have seen in this message is a higher vision concerning the church. We have seen that Eve as the wife of Adam is a type of the church as the wife of Christ. Just as Eve was a pure product out of Adam so the church must be a pure product out of Christ. Someone may ask how the church today could be such an Eve, a pure product out of Christ. This is why we all need to see the vision. When you see the vision, you are Eve. Without the vision, it would be hard for you to be Eve. All things other than the pure element of Christ are ruled out by this vision. This is why we should not remain under the influence of the traditional teachings. We need the vision. When we see the vision that the church is in resurrection, in Christ, and in the heavenlies, it will rule out everything other than Christ, resurrection, and the heavenlies.

We all need to praise, thank, and worship the Lord for His mercy in showing us such a vision. It is absolutely the Lord's mercy that He has opened up His Word to us in such a way. The light we have received from the Lord's holy Word is nothing but His mercy.

CHAPTER FOUR

THE VISION CONCERNING
THE KINGDOM

THE LIFE OF GOD—
OUR ENTRANCE INTO THE KINGDOM OF GOD

The kingdom is a great and difficult subject. We must realize that any kind of life is a kingdom. The plant life is the plant kingdom, the animal life is the animal kingdom, the human life is the human kingdom, and the divine life is the divine kingdom. A life is always a kingdom. The life of God is the kingdom of God. If you want to enter into a kingdom, you need that kingdom's particular life. If you want to enter into the botanic kingdom, you need the botanic life. If you want to enter into the animal kingdom, you need the animal life. We human beings are all in the human kingdom because we were born into it—we have the human life. The human life is our entrance into the human kingdom. In the same principle, John 3:5 tells us that we must be born of the Spirit, which means we are born with the divine life, God's life, the uncreated eternal life. Then we can enter into the kingdom of God. The life of God is our entrance into the kingdom of God. We must see this basic principle. When most Christian teachers touch this matter of the kingdom, they do not see this basic principle.

THE KINGDOM AND THE CHURCH

Now we must see the difference or the relationship between the kingdom and the church. This is very hard to discern and to understand clearly. We have seen that any kind of life is a kingdom, so the kingdom is the life itself.

The kingdom of God is the life of God, but the church is not the life, nor is the life the church. The church is the product of life. The divine life is the kingdom and this life produces the church. The New Testament concept is that the gospel brings in the kingdom. The gospel does not bring in the church, but the gospel brings forth the church. Thus, the gospel brings in the kingdom of God, and the gospel also brings forth the church of God. This is why the gospel is called the gospel of the kingdom in the New Testament (Matt. 4:23; 9:35; 24:14). There is not a verse in the New Testament that tells us that the gospel is the gospel of the church. The gospel of the kingdom brings forth, produces, the church because the kingdom is the life itself and the church is the issue, the produce, of life. As you can see, the kingdom and the church are very closely related. The New Testament refers to the preaching of the gospel of peace (Eph. 2:17). This peace produces the church. No verse, however, tells us to preach the church. The Bible also tells us to preach forgiveness of sins (Luke 24:47) and to preach the gospel of the kingdom, but never to preach the church because the church is the product of what is preached.

The Lord told Peter in Matthew 16:18-19 that He would build His church upon the revelation of Christ which Peter had received from the Father. Immediately after this the Lord said to Peter, "I will give to you the keys of the kingdom of the heavens" (v. 19). Without the kingdom as the reality of life, the church could never be produced or built up. To produce the church and to build up the church, we need the kingdom. The kingdom actually is the reality of the church. We cannot say, however, that the church is the reality of the kingdom. We can only say that the kingdom is the reality of the church.

With this understanding as a basis, we can understand many verses in the New Testament. The first preaching of the New Testament gospel told people that they needed to repent because the kingdom of the heavens had drawn near (Matt. 3:2; 4:17; 10:7). There is no verse that says the church is coming, so repent. John the Baptist, Jesus, and the twelve apostles initiated the New Testament gospel by telling people that the kingdom had drawn near. This meant that the time had come for God to come to dispense Himself as life to people. The gospel brings God as life, and life is a kingdom. The kingdom is the realm of life for life to move, to work, to rule, and to govern that life may accomplish its purpose and this realm is the kingdom. Actually, the kingdom as the realm of life is life itself. If one were to take away all the animals in the zoo, there would be no animal kingdom there. When the animals are there, the animal life is there and that realm of animal life is the animal kingdom. The gospel brings in the divine life and the divine life has its realm for it to move, to work, to rule, and to govern that this life may accomplish its purpose. This is the kingdom, and this divine life with its realm produces the church.

THE KINGDOM SEED

Mark 4:26 says that the kingdom is like a seed sown into the earth. The kingdom is the seed and the seed is the seed of the divine life (1 John 3:9; 1 Pet. 1:23). When the Lord says the kingdom is like a seed, that means the kingdom is the life. The kingdom grows like a seed grows and the kingdom develops like a seed by its growing until it develops unto a harvest. Matthew 13 also shows us that the kingdom is like a seed sown into the human earth and that this seed grows in our heart to be the kingdom (vv. 8, 23). Now we can understand why in Luke 17 when the Pharisees asked the Lord when the kingdom of God would come, He told them that the kingdom of God was among them. This indicated that Jesus, He Himself, is the kingdom because He is the seed.

In 1972 in a summer conference in Los Angeles, I gave messages on the kingdom. In those messages I indicated that the kingdom is the "King" plus "dom." Jesus is the King. When Jesus expands, He becomes the kingdom. The

King plus the dom is the kingdom. The preposition among in Luke 17:21 where Jesus told the Pharisees that the kingdom of God was among them can also be translated into within. The kingdom of God is within you. Both of these translations are right. At that time Jesus, the seed of the kingdom, was sown among the Jewish people and He was also sown into some of them like Peter, James, and John; the kingdom was not only among them but was also within them. According to the Pharisees, however, the kingdom at that time was only among them. This kingdom is Jesus as the seed of life sown into humanity.

A CLEAR UNDERSTANDING OF JOHN 3:5

Now we should be able to have a clear understanding of John 3:5. For years I could not understand why regeneration had something to do with entering into the kingdom of God. Then I began to see that regeneration is to receive the divine life and that this divine life is our entrance into the divine life's kingdom. You must have this divine life; otherwise, there is no way for you to enter into its kingdom. If a chicken or tiger wanted to enter into the human kingdom, they would have to be reborn, to be regenerated with the human life. Once they received the human life, that human life would become their entry into the human kingdom. In the same principle, if we want to enter into the kingdom of God, we need to be born of the life of God. Once we have the life of God, this life is our entrance into the kingdom of God.

THE KINGDOM NOT BEING SUSPENDED

After the Lord's resurrection, the book of Acts tells us that the Lord stayed with the disciples for forty days and in those forty days He taught the disciples concerning the kingdom of God (1:3). Some brethren teachers and Dr. C. I. Scofield, in their teachings regarding the kingdom held the concept that the Lord Jesus presented the kingdom to the Jews and the Jews rejected it. Therefore, He suspended this kingdom and put the kingdom aside. Then He began to touch the church. With this understanding as a basis, they say that today is not the kingdom age but the age of the church. To them, when the Lord comes back He will receive the kingdom from God and He will come back with this kingdom based upon Luke 19:11-12, 15 and Daniel 7:13-14. By that time the Jewish people will repent and believe in Him and will receive this kingdom brought back by the Lord Jesus. Then there will be the next age, the age of the kingdom. This concept is very much in contradiction with the Acts, the Epistles, and Revelation.

The Kingdom in the Acts

The Acts shows us strongly that the Lord Jesus never gave up the kingdom and never put it aside to come to the matter of the church. Rather, after His resurrection He stayed with His disciples for forty days purposely to show them the kingdom of God. Acts 8:12 tells us that Philip the evangelist went out to preach the kingdom of God and in Acts 14:22 Paul charged the saints that through many tribulations they must enter into the kingdom of God. Also, at the end of Acts (28:30-31) Paul stayed in Rome in a rented house for the purpose of preaching the kingdom of God both to the Jews and to the Gentiles. In our concept, we always consider that in the Acts the gospel was preached only for the purpose of producing and establishing the churches. We never thought that the gospel had much to do with the kingdom.

The Gospel of the Kingdom

In Luke and Acts, Luke uses the word "evangelize." Evangelize is the anglicized form of the Greek word *euaggelizo*, which means to preach something as the gospel. In Luke 4:43 Luke tells us that the Lord said that He had to evangelize the kingdom of God. This means to preach the kingdom of God as the gospel. The verb evangelize implies the noun, the gospel. To evangelize the kingdom means to preach the kingdom as the gospel. We cannot find a verse which says to evangelize the church, to preach the church as the gospel. Whatever was preached in the Acts was the preaching of the kingdom of God as the gospel. This is why the gospel is called the gospel of the kingdom of God. The gospel of the kingdom of God equals the gospel. The gospel of the kingdom of God equals the gospel of life because life is the kingdom and the kingdom is the life in the realm for the life to move, to work, to rule, and to govern.

The Kingdom as Our Life and Inheritance

Then in the Epistles, in 1 Corinthians (6:9-10; 15:50), Galatians (5:21), Ephesians (5:5), and Colossians (1:13; 4:11), the kingdom of God is referred to strongly. You must live a life that is according to the Spirit. You must live a life that is Christ Himself. Otherwise, you will not inherit the kingdom of God. You need to live a life which is the kingdom today. Then this life will qualify you to enter into the coming kingdom. Today the kingdom is your life and in the next age the kingdom will become your inheritance. What you live today will become your inheritance tomorrow. For example, what you earn in wages today is your living. Then these earnings will become your coming social security. In like manner, you must live the kingdom and then the kingdom will become your coming social security. That is the coming kingdom as an inheritance to all who live the kingdom as their life.

The Reality of the Church Life

Romans 14:17 says, "For the kingdom of God is not eating and drinking, but righteousness and peace and joy in the Holy Spirit." Romans 14 teaches us about the practical church life—how to receive the weaker believers without any kind of division. In that chapter on the church life, Paul says that the kingdom is this practical church life. Also, in Revelation 1 John stressed the church as the lampstands for the testimony of Jesus (vv. 2, 9, 12, 20). In Revelation 1:9, however, John did not say, "I John, your brother in the church" but he said, "I John, your brother in the kingdom." When he was in the church life he was in the kingdom because the kingdom is the reality of the church life.

The kingdom is the practical life, life's practicality. Again, I refer to the example of the zoo where we can see an animal kingdom. The animal kingdom is the practicality of the animal life. If we live the divine life, if we live Christ as life, the practicality of this life is the kingdom. When people come among us they would see a kingdom. The kingdom is the expression of life. All the animals moving around in the zoo are an expression of the animal life and that expression is the animal kingdom. If all the animals were taken away, the animal life would be over and the expression would also be over. In the church, we are the believers living, moving, and acting in the divine life. As a result, there is an expression of this divine life. The expression of this divine life is the kingdom, the practicality of this life, and the practicality of this divine life is in the church. Now we can see that the kingdom is the reality of the church life. As long as the divine life is here, the kingdom is here. As long as the divine life is being lived, the kingdom exists. You could never suspend it and you could never put it aside.

THE REALITY, THE APPEARANCE, AND THE MANIFESTATION OF THE KINGDOM OF THE HEAVENS

In the Gospel of Matthew, the Lord's teaching on the mount in chapters five through seven, His parables by the seashore in chapter thirteen, and His prophecy on the Mount of Olives in chapters twenty-four and twenty-five, when added together, unveil to us the entire situation of the kingdom. His teaching in Matthew 5 through 7 shows us the reality of the kingdom of the heavens, His parables in Matthew 13 show us the appearance of the kingdom of the heavens, and His prophecy in Matthew 24 and 25 shows us the manifestation of the kingdom of the heavens.

The Reality

First, this kingdom has its reality and this reality is the living of the divine life. Matthew 5 through 7 is not a matter of morality or a high standard of ethics but the living of the divine life by the believers. The living of the divine life is the expression and the practicality of the divine life, so it is the kingdom in reality. We must be impressed that Matthew 5 through 7 is not a sermon on a high standard of ethics. It is the unveiling of the living of the divine life which we possess. This living is the expression, the practicality of the divine life, which is the divine life's kingdom, the reality of the kingdom.

The Appearance

In Matthew 13:24-42 the appearance of the kingdom of the heavens is revealed in the parable of the tares, of the mustard seed, and of the leaven. In Matthew 13 the evil one is portrayed as the birds in the air (vv. 4, 19). Chapter thirteen also tells us clearly that this enemy is the Devil (v. 39). While this kingdom is going on on the earth, Satan endeavors to do everything to frustrate the growth and development of this kingdom.

The Tares

First, Satan sowed the tares among the wheat to frustrate the life of the wheat from growing. This is the appearance of the kingdom of the heavens which is full of tares, full of nominal, false Christians. These false Christians many times are very hard to discern. It is not possible to discern tares from the wheat until the fruit is produced. The sprout and leaves of the tares look the same as those of the wheat. When the fruit is produced, though, the wheat bears golden colored grain, but the fruit of the tares is black. When the fruit is produced you can discern

what is real and what is false. Sometimes even among us
things may be like this. Before the fruit is produced we all
look alike, but one day some will become golden and some
will become black and there will be no need to discern. By
that time the growth of life with the wheat will have been
greatly frustrated by the tares. Wheat signifies all the
believers of the divine life and with the divine life. The
tares were sown by the enemy to frustrate the proper
growth of this divine life in the believers. Nevertheless, the
wheat still grows with the divine life and produces the
grain to be ground into powder. This is the fine flour
(13:33) to make a loaf (1 Cor. 10:16-17) for an offering to
God, which means to make the church as a total offering to
God for His enjoyment and satisfaction.

The Leaven

The church, as the practical kingdom of the heavens,
with Christ—the unleavened fine flour—as its content,
must be the unleavened bread (1 Cor. 5:7-8). Then the
enemy endeavored to put leaven into this fine flour until
the fine flour was altogether leavened (13:33). Once the
flour is leavened there is no way to purge it, no way to
purify it. We all must realize that we are still under a
certain kind or a certain extent of leavening. All the truths
we have heard and received in the past have been leavened
by the enemy. If this were not the case it would not be so
hard for us to minister the Word. Even the seeking
Christians today do not realize how much their mentality
has been preoccupied already by the leavened truth. Even
before people get saved they have already become leavened
by the practices, by the atmosphere, by the color, and by
the flavor of Christianity. After they were saved, many of
these leavened truths still remained in their mentality.

The Mustard Seed

The parable of the mustard seed (13:31-32) shows us
that Satan is very subtle. He not only sows the tares

among the wheat and puts the leaven into the fine flour, but he also is even able to change the principle of life to make the mustard seed grow not according to its kind. According to the law of God's creation, every plant must be after its kind (Gen. 1:11-12). Satan, however, made the mustard seed to grow not after its own kind. It should be an herb to produce the proper food for people, but Satan made it a tree to become a lodging for so many birds. Now this tree lodges many evil persons and things. The nature of the mustard seed has been changed. It is no more an herb to feed people but a tree to lodge so many birds. This great tree is today's Christendom.

This is all the appearance of the kingdom of the heavens: many tares, a great tree as a lodging for evil persons and evil things, and much leaven. In today's Christendom we can see tares, leaven, and a great tree. We do not see much fine flour.

The Manifestation

Then when the Lord Jesus comes the kingdom will be manifested. This is the manifestation of the kingdom of the heavens. Those who will enjoy the manifestation of the kingdom of the heavens are those who are now living in the reality of the kingdom. If we live the kingdom today, the kingdom will be our inheritance as a realm for us to enter in and enjoy the eternal life for a thousand years as the reward with its joy and kingship (Matt. 24:45-47; 25:19-23).

This kingdom in the next age will be the heavenly part of the millennium, and the earthly part will be the restored tabernacle of David (Acts 15:16), the restored kingdom of Israel (Acts 1:6). The saved remnant of the Jews in the restored Davidic kingdom will be the priests teaching the nations to worship God (Zech. 8:20-23). The kings, the overcoming believers, are not in the restored Davidic kingdom, but they are in the manifestation of the kingdom in the heavenly part of the millennium (Rev. 20:4, 6).

We should not forget that a number of God's chosen and redeemed people in the time of the patriarchs, the dispensation before the law, were not perfected. Also, a great number of God's chosen ones in the dispensation of law and a greater number of God's chosen ones in the dispensation of grace were not mature before the millennium, the fourth dispensation, the dispensation of the kingdom. As a result, all these immature ones will be perfected in the fourth dispensation, and the perfection will not be so pleasant. That perfection will be a kind of discipline or punishment to force you to "make up your lesson" to grow into maturity.

Then all these will be mature and God's work to perfect His chosen and redeemed ones will be completed. This will be the end of the old creation, and the new heaven and the new earth will come in. At that time all of the believers who needed perfecting in the millennium, the overcoming believers in the heavenly part of the millennium, and the Jews who were the priests to teach the nations will be completely perfected and matured. They will be the complete kingdom of God for eternity because all of them will be full of life, and this life is the consummation of the kingdom of God, which will be the New Jerusalem. The New Jerusalem will be the eternal kingdom of God for eternity.

CHAPTER FIVE

THE VISION CONCERNING THE NEW JERUSALEM— THE ULTIMATE CONSUMMATION

(1)

We must have a clear view about the entire Bible. The Bible, comprised of sixty-six holy books, is the divine revelation. The New Jerusalem is the conclusion of such a great book. Also, in this great book, God's economy, His eternal purpose, His eternal plan, is fully revealed with His divine purpose, which is the highest purpose in the universe. The New Jerusalem is the conclusion of this purpose, of this plan, of this economy.

THE TOTAL CONCLUSION OF THE BIBLE

We must also see that none of the sixty-six books of the Bible has an adequate conclusion. Genesis does not have one. This book is concluded with a dead man in a coffin, buried in Egypt (50:26). Is that a satisfactory conclusion? Then the book of Exodus concludes with something glorious, which is quite in contrast to the conclusion of Genesis—a tabernacle filled with God's glory (40:34). Even though this conclusion is glorious, it is still not adequate. Matthew concludes with a kind of commission. The Lord charges the disciples to go to disciple the nations and baptize them into the Triune God (28:19-20). Again, this is not an adequate conclusion. The book of John concludes with the matter of fishing (21:1-14) and in the Acts we could not see an actual conclusion. The last verse of Acts says that Paul was "proclaiming the kingdom of God, and teaching the things concerning the Lord Jesus Christ with all boldness, unhindered" (28:31). Only one book of the sixty-six books of the Bible, Revelation, has the conclusion of the Bible, because all of the sixty-six books are concluded with one item—the New Jerusalem. The New Jerusalem is the total conclusion of the sixty-six books, the entire, total conclusion of the Bible.

THE CONSUMMATION OF ALL THE ITEMS IN THE BIBLE

The New Jerusalem is not only the conclusion to the entire Bible, but also the consummation of all the items in the Bible. The Triune God, His economy, Christ's redemption, God's salvation, the believers, the church, and the kingdom all consummate in this one item—the New Jerusalem. It is imperative that we see that the New Jerusalem is the ultimate consummation of all the subjects, the items, the matters, the persons, and the things recorded in the holy writings. As the consummation, it is an exceedingly great item.

Based upon these few points which I have mentioned, we can realize that the New Jerusalem surely could never be a physical mansion for God's redeemed to lodge in for eternity. It is too low to say this. This is like the conclusion of a kindergarten text book. Surely the holy writings as the entire revelation of the great, purposeful God would not end in this way. The New Jerusalem must be the consummation of the Triune God with His economy and the consummation of the wonderful church and the marvelous kingdom. The significance of this consummation must fit all these points. From the entire divine revelation of the Bible we must infer logically that the New Jerusalem surely could never be a physical, lodging place. We must be impressed that the New Jerusalem is the consummation of all the divine items in the Bible. Although this consummation only occupies a little over one chapter in the Bible, it comprises every basic, intrinsic, essential, and genuine item in the entire divine revelation. We must see this.

NOT A PHYSICAL MANSION

In order to understand the New Jerusalem properly, I would like to present six reasons why the New Jerusalem could not be a physical mansion.

A Book of Signs

First, we must realize that the first verse of the book of Revelation tells us how this book was written: "The revelation of Jesus Christ which God gave to Him to show to His slaves what must swiftly take place; and He made it known by signs" (Rev. 1:1). This verse tells us that the Lord Jesus made this God-given revelation known to us by signs. It would help us to circle, color, or underline the word "signs" in this verse. The Lord Jesus made this revelation known to us by signs. The word signs is the key word to interpret the entire book of Revelation. Revelation is a book of signs. Every number in the book of Revelation is a sign. Seven is a sign, four is a sign, twelve is a sign, and ten is a sign. The lampstands (1:11-13, 20) are signs. The Lamb who was slain (5:6) is a sign. The lion (5:5) is a sign. The seven stars (1:16, 20) are signs. In 4:3 the One who was sitting on the throne looks like jasper. Jasper is also a sign. In Revelation 12:1 the universal woman crowned with twelve stars, clothed with the sun, and standing on the moon is a great sign. Could such a wonderful woman be merely a single, individualistic female? It is not logical to interpret it in this way. Also in Revelation 12 is a great red dragon (v. 3). This is also a sign, as well as the man-child (v. 5). Then in the next chapter, chapter thirteen, we see the beast coming out of the Mediterranean Sea (vv. 1-2). That beast signifies the coming Caesar of the coming Roman Empire. It is a sign of a man (v. 18). The harvest in Revelation 14:15 is also a sign, signifying God's living people. The firstfruit in Revelation 14:4 is a sign which signifies the living overcomers among God's living people. The number one hundred forty-four thousand is also a sign (v. 1). The glassy sea in 15:2 is another sign. Then in chapter seventeen we see a great prostitute (v. 1), Babylon the Great (v. 5). This surely will not be a physical city of Babylon which is today's Baghdad in Iraq. The great Babylon, the mystery, is a sign in Revelation 17. In chapter 19 we see a bride, the wife of the Lamb, who is clothed with righteousness (vv. 7-8). Do you believe that when the Lord Jesus comes back He will marry a literal woman, a single female? To interpret the signs in the Bible in this way is seriously wrong. I hope we can see all the signs in this book. What is the last sign, then, of this book of signs? The last sign of this book, which is made known to us mainly by signs, is the New Jerusalem.

Not Logical

The second reason that we could not say that the New Jerusalem is a physical mansion or a physical city for God's redeemed people to lodge in is that it is altogether not logical to say this. The New Jerusalem, the holy city, is a golden mountain (Rev. 21:16, 18). This mountain is twelve thousand stadia in three dimensions. The length, the breadth, and the height of the city are twelve thousand stadia (v. 16). Twelve thousand stadia is about thirteen-hundred and fifty miles, the approximate distance from New York to Dallas. Such a high mountain has only one street which goes down spirally from the top of the mountain to reach all the twelve gates on the four sides of the city. If this is a real city to lodge in, we must ask how all God's redeemed through all the centuries will be able to lodge there. How could so many people live in a city with only one main spiral street? How could these people travel in a city with only one main street?

We have seen that the book of Revelation was written in the way of signs. If you say that the last sign, the New Jerusalem, is a physical, real city, then what about the lampstands as the first sign in this book? Are the seven stars in chapter one real stars? And what about the Lamb?

Do you believe Christ as the Lamb of God is an actual lamb with four legs and a little tail? Is the lion of the tribe of Judah a real lion like one at the zoo? It is not logical to interpret these signs in the book of Revelation in this way. The New Jerusalem is a sign. It is not a genuine, real, physical city. The great Babylon is also a sign of the false church. The great Babylon and the New Jerusalem are two signs at the end of the book of Revelation. One city is a sign of the false church and the other city, the holy city, signifies the ultimate consummation of the pure church. The great Babylon is called the great prostitute. The New Jerusalem is called the wife of the Lamb. Since Revelation is a book written with signs, the New Jerusalem could not be an exception; it must be a sign.

The Wife of the Lamb

The third reason why the New Jerusalem could not be a physical mansion is that Revelation itself tells us that this city is the wife of the Lamb (21:9). According to the entire Bible there is a divine romance between God the Creator, the Redeemer, who is the male, and His redeemed people who are the female. This is a basic thing revealed in the Bible. In the Old Testament God told His redeemed people Israel that He was their husband and that they were His wife (Isa. 54:5; Jer. 3:14; 31:32; Hosea 2:19). When the Lord Jesus came, John the Baptist told his disciples that Christ was the bridegroom coming to take the bride which is the church (John 3:29). Then Paul tells us in Ephesians 5 that the church is typified by the wife and Christ is typified by the husband (vv. 24-25). Therefore, Christ is the husband and the church is the wife. Paul also said, that he had betrothed us as a virgin to one husband (2 Cor. 11:2) who is Christ. Also, Revelation 19:7 says, "The marriage of the Lamb is come, and His wife has made herself ready." This wife is the aggregate of all the overcoming saints from Abel until the Lord comes back. The aggregate of all the Old Testament overcomers and the New Testament overcomers is the wife in Revelation 19:7 who will be ready for Christ's wedding. The New Jerusalem is the consummation of God's counterpart, the aggregate of all His redeemed and perfected people. In the Bible, beginning from Adam and Eve (Ephesians 5 indicates that Adam and Eve were a type of Christ and the church) to the end of the book of Revelation, there are many portions of the Scripture which reveal that God is the universal husband and His redeemed and perfected people are the universal counterpart to match God. Such a revelation needs a consummation and the consummation is the New Jerusalem as the wife of the Redeemer, the Lamb, Christ, the embodiment of the Triune God.

The Consummation
of the Tabernacle and the Temple

The fourth reason that the New Jerusalem is not a physical building is that Revelation tells us that the New Jerusalem is God's tabernacle (21:3) and also that the New Jerusalem is the temple of God (21:22). John said that he did not see a temple in the city for its temple was the Lord God the Almighty and the Lamb. The tabernacle in the type of the Old Testament was not only the dwelling place of God, but also the dwelling place of all His serving priests. The serving priests who served God dwelt with God in the tabernacle. Therefore, the tabernacle is a dwelling place for God and His serving ones. In Revelation 22:3 we are told that all the redeemed and perfected saints in eternity will be God's serving ones. Therefore, they all will dwell in the tabernacle with God. According to typology the tabernacle was a precursor of the temple which brought in the temple. John did not see the temple, but God and the Lamb were the temple, which indicates that God and the Lamb became the dwelling place of His serving ones. This word matches Psalm 90:1 which says, "Lord, thou hast been our dwelling place in all generations." Therefore, the tabernacle is God's dwelling place with His serving ones and this very God who dwells in the tabernacle is the temple which is the dwelling place of His serving ones. Again, we must realize what a wrong concept it is to say that the New Jerusalem is a great physical mansion for God's children to lodge in. Revelation says that God Himself, God and the Lamb, will be the temple for us who serve Him to dwell in. Our dwelling place in eternity is God Himself. We must stress this strongly. God and the Lamb will be the temple in eternity for His people, His serving ones, to dwell in. We will not dwell in a big mansion. We will dwell in God. Hallelujah! He is our temple and we are His tabernacle. He dwells in us and we dwell in Him and this mutual dwelling is the New Jerusalem which to God is the tabernacle and to us is the temple.

We must realize that the entire Bible is a history of the tabernacle and the temple. Beginning in Exodus 25 we see the tabernacle, which became the center of Old Testament history. Then this tabernacle entered into the good land and was replaced by the temple which continued to be the center of Old Testament history through the book of Malachi. The Old Testament then is a history of the tabernacle and the temple. In the New Testament, firstly the Lord Jesus was the tabernacle in John 1:14 and He was also the temple in John 2:19-22. In John 2 He indicated that in His resurrection this temple would be enlarged to be a corporate temple, which is the church (1 Cor. 3:16; Eph. 2:21). Therefore, the tabernacle and the temple are also the center of the New Testament history. The entire Bible is a book of the tabernacle and the temple. This needs a consummation. The consummation of the tabernacle and the temple is the New Jerusalem because the New Jerusalem will be the eternal tabernacle for God and will be the eternal temple for us. It is the consummation of the tabernacle and temple in the Bible.

The Consummation of God's Building

Now we come to the fifth reason. The Bible is a book of

building. First, God charged Noah to build the ark. Then we see in the Old Testament that Abraham was looking for a city and that his descendants, the children of Israel, built a tabernacle. Later, they entered into the good land and built a temple. In the New Testament the Lord said that He would build His church (Matt. 16:18). He also told the Jews in John 2:19 that if they would destroy "this temple," referring to the temple of His body, He would raise it up in three days. Even Peter rebuked the Jews by saying that they, the builders, had rejected Christ as the cornerstone of God's building (Acts 4:11). Also, Paul told us that we are the house of God (1 Tim. 3:15) and that we are God's building (1 Cor. 3:9). Paul as the wise master builder laid the foundation, and we have to build upon the foundation, taking heed not to build with wood, grass, and stubble, but with gold, silver, and precious stones (1 Cor. 3:10-12). Then Peter told us in his first Epistle that Christ is the living stone for God's building and we are like Him as the living stones to be built up into a spiritual house (1 Pet. 2:4-5). We can see that God's building is a line throughout the entire Bible, and the consummation of this building is the New Jerusalem.

The Consummation of
All That God Is and Has Achieved

Now we must see the final reason why the New Jerusalem could not be interpreted as a physical mansion. Our God is the great Triune God—the Father, the Son, and the Spirit. The Father has an eternal plan with a marvelous economy and the Son accomplished this economy by becoming incarnated, by His living on this earth, by His dying an all-inclusive death, and by His entering into resurrection and ascension. The Son's achievements were excellent, marvelous, and very meaningful. Then the Spirit came to apply all that the Son had accomplished to us. The Spirit worked to regenerate us and is now working within us to transform us, to redeem our body, to transfigure us, to make us just like Christ. By all these the church will be produced and built up and there will be a kingdom for the overcomers of God's chosen people to rule the world with Christ. The great Triune God with all of His achievements and workings throughout the ages surely needs a marvelous consummation. Could a physical city as a lodging place be a consummation of all these achievements? Absolutely not. The consummation of all that God is and has achieved and accomplished is the New Jerusalem. These six reasons show us that the New Jerusalem could not be a physical mansion or a physical city for God's redeemed people to lodge in.

THE ULTIMATE CONSUMMATION

If any one would not accept this vision, how could he answer our questions concerning the New Jerusalem as a sign of the wife as a consummation of all the females in the Bible typifying God's counterpart, and of the tabernacle of God as a consummation of all the tabernacles and temples in the entire Bible? How could he answer the questions concerning the building in the Bible needing a consummation, and the great God with His great economy and with all His great achievements needing an ultimate consummation? Without the New Jerusalem, there is no consummation to all these things. And how could he explain how a physical lodging place could contain billions of God's redeemed people? I do not think anyone could answer these questions. And I do hope that these questions and the fellowship we have had would convince and subdue all of us. We must take this conclusion—that the New Jerusalem as the conclusion of the entire Bible is the ultimate consummation of God's great planned economy and great achievements.

The consummation is a living composition of all God's chosen, redeemed, regenerated, transformed, and glorified people. Such a living composition, with many wonderful living persons, is the consummation of the entire Bible, and this composition is a mutual abiding, a mutual dwelling, a mutual habitation. God inhabits His redeemed people and His redeemed people inhabit Him. His redeemed people as a composition will be His tabernacle and He and the Lamb will be their temple. This is marvelous, meaningful, and very significant.

THE CONTENTS OF THE NEW JERUSALEM

Now we must see the contents of the New Jerusalem. From the throne of God and of the Lamb in the center of the city flows a river of water of life and in this river of life grows the tree of life. Also, the entire city is enlightened by the light of life. These three items are the intrinsic essence of the Triune God. The intrinsic essence of the Triune God is the divine life. The divine life will be the river (22:1), the divine life will be the tree (22:2), and the divine life will be the light (22:5). We will drink the river, we will eat the tree, and we will live in the light. These three items are of the intrinsic and basic essence of the Triune God. The light mainly denotes God the Father. Revelation tells us that in the New Jerusalem there is no need of the light of a lamp or of the sun because the Lord God will be the light and Christ the Lamb will be the lamp (21:23). The tree of life refers to God the Son and the river of water of life refers to God the Spirit. This is the divine Trinity in the divine essence for our living and enjoyment in eternity.

The basic, intrinsic essence of the New Jerusalem is the divine life. The divine life with God the Father is the light, with God the Son is the tree, and with God the Spirit is the river. The light is for us to live in, the tree is for us to feed on, and the river is for us to drink of. This will be our living and our enjoyment of the intrinsic essence of the Triune God for eternity, and He will abide in us and we will abide in Him. There is a miniature of this mutual abiding in John 15: "Abide in Me and I in you" (15:4). This abiding in John 15 will be expanded and developed into the New Jerusalem, which will be the consummation of the divine mutual abiding. We abide in Him and He abides in us for eternity. We will serve Him and He will be served by us, and this will be the eternal kingdom, the eternal realm of the divine life.

This is the consummation of the entire Bible of all that God is and of all that God has accomplished, achieved, and attained. This is our vision. This is the typical, genuine, proper, unique eschatology. Praise the Lord for such an eschatology. The Triune God and all of His chosen and redeemed people will be part of this unique consummation.

CHAPTER SIX

THE VISION CONCERNING THE NEW JERUSALEM— THE ULTIMATE CONSUMMATION

(2)

We still need to see more of the vision concerning the New Jerusalem. We must see that this vision is concerning the ultimate consummation of the entire revelation of God, of the entire Bible, and of the entire Triune God with all His plan, economy, and all His achievements. In this message I want to point out how we can apply this ultimate consummation to the facts in the Bible.

THE NAMES OF THE TWELVE TRIBES AND OF THE TWELVE APOSTLES

First, this New Jerusalem is a composition of the Old Testament saints, represented by the twelve tribes (Rev. 21:12), and the New Testament saints, represented by the twelve apostles (Rev. 21:14). The Old Testament is a history of the twelve tribes and the New Testament is a history of the twelve apostles. Therefore, when these twenty-four names are put on this composition, this indicates that this compostion is an ultimate consummation of the history of the twelve tribes and of the history of the twelve apostles. In other words, if we are going to understand the items of the twelve names of the twelve tribes we need to understand the entire Old Testament. Also, if we are going to understand the names of the twelve apostles we need to understand the entire New Testament. These twenty-four names on this composition are a part of the ultimate consummation of the things in the Bible.

The names of the twelve tribes on the twelve gates (Rev. 21:12-13, 21a) indicate that the history of the twelve tribes is a kind of entering. The law, which comprises a major part of the Old Testament, is considered by Paul as a child-conductor which conducted us to Christ (Gal. 3:24). We may say that the entire Old Testament history of the twelve tribes is a kind of conducting business. The Old Testament conducted us to Christ. Now Christ is "the oyster" which produces the pearls to be the gates of this New Jerusalem. Actually, the twelve tribes conducted us to Christ, the One who produces the pearl through His death and through His resurrection. His death fulfilled all the obligations of the Old Testament. By fulfilling the obligations of the Old Testament His death terminated the Old Testament and stopped it. Paul's thought in Galatians 3 was that after the law conducted God's chosen people to Christ, Christ's death stopped the law by fulfilling it. The death of Christ stopped the Old Testament and the resurrection of Christ began the New Testament by His life secreting to produce the pearls which are the very entry into this ultimate consummation. Christ's dying to fulfill the obligations of the Old Testament stopped the Old Testament and terminated it. He secreted His life juice in His resurrection to produce the precious pearls which are the three-fold entries on the four sides of the holy city. Thus, the twelve gates of twelve pearls bearing the names of the twelve tribes of Israel signify the ultimate consummation of the Old Testament.

Then we see the twelve names of the twelve apostles on the twelve foundations of the city (Rev. 21:14, 19-20). Whatever was there in the Old Testament was a kind of conducting, a kind of entry, but whatever is in the New Testament is a foundation. Whoever has been conducted to Christ will be led to the New Testament foundation. This one must be built upon the foundation of the New Testament signified by the twelve names of the apostles. This foundation is the ultimate consummation of the entire

New Testament. Ephesians 2:20 tells us that the church is built upon the foundation of the apostles and the prophets. This means that their teaching and their speaking forth of Christ laid a foundation. The Old Testament was a conducting to the gates and the New Testament is a foundation for this ultimate consummation.

THE ULTIMATE CONSUMMATION
OF THE TRIUNE GOD

Now we must see that the ultimate consummation of the Triune God in this consummation is at least five-fold.

Our Entrance

First, the Triune God is the entrance into the holy city. The "three gates" on each side (Rev. 21:13) signify that the Triune God—Father, Son, and Spirit—work together to bring people into the holy city. This is indicated in the three parables in Luke 15 and implied in the Lord's word in Matthew 28:19. To be baptized into the Father, the Son, and the Spirit is the real entrance into the holy city.

Our Constitution

Second, the substances of the Triune God are the building materials of this New Jerusalem. Gold signifies God the Father's nature (Rev. 21:18b, 21b), pearls signify the produce of Christ through His death and resurrection (Rev 21:21a), and precious stones signify the transforming work of the Spirit (Rev. 21:18a, 19-20). These are the three-fold materials for the building up of the New Jerusalem. This ultimate consummation is constituted with the Father's nature as the gold, with the Son's produce as the pearl, and with the Spirit's work as the precious stones. These are the essences of the constitution of this ultimate consummation. Therefore, this New Jerusalem is the ultimate consummation of the Triune God in His essence to be the constituting elements of this ultimate consummation.

Our Enjoyment

Third, as we have seen already, in this ultimate consummation the divine life in its three-foldness is the very enjoyment of God's redeemed in eternity forever. The divine life is the river for God's redeemed to drink of (Rev. 22:1, 17), the divine life is the tree for God's redeemed to feed on for their living and for their enjoyment (Rev. 22:2a, 14, 19), and the divine life is the light for God's redeemed to live in (Rev. 21:23, 11). This is another aspect of the ultimate consummation of the Triune God as the divine life for the enjoyment and living of His redeemed ones. The gospel of John also shows us that the Triune God in this age is our enjoyment in a three-fold way. He is our living water (John 7:37-39; 4:10, 13-14), He is our bread (John 6:48), and He is our light (John 8:12). These three items are in John for our present enjoyment and living, and this will consummate in the New Jerusalem as the divine river satisfying us, the divine tree feeding us, and the divine light enlightening us. This is the ultimate consummation of the divine life of the Triune God for His redeemed people's enjoyment and living forever.

Our Living

Fourth, in the entire city there is only one street (Rev. 22:1). The street of gold (21:21) signifies that the Father's nature is our way, our street, our route for our traffic, for our fellowship, and for our move. The Father's nature is the golden street for His people to travel, to fellowship. The river of water of life proceeds in the middle of this street and the tree of life grows on the two sides of the river (22:1-2). The Son is the tree of life so the tree of life signifies the Son's being, which is the food of God's redeemed people. The river of water of life is the Spirit's flowing and this flowing is the reaching application. Thus, in the holy city we see the Father's nature, the Son's being, and the Spirit's application. We walk in the Father's nature, we feed on the

Son's being, and we drink of the Spirit's availability. This is another aspect of the ultimate consummation of the Trinity.

Our Being, Our Existence

Let us go on to consider the fifth aspect of the ultimate consummation of the Trinity. In Revelation 22 we see the throne on which God and the Lamb *is* sitting (vv. 1, 3). I do not use the predicate *are* but I use the verb *is* purposely because God and the Lamb are not two but one. The Lamb is the lamp and God is the light within Him (21:23; 22:5). Proceeding out of the throne is the river of water of life. God signifies the Creator and the Lamb signifies the Redeemer sitting on the throne. Out of the very God and the very Lamb who sit on the throne flows the river of water of life which signifies the Spirit as the Regenerator. God created, the Lamb redeemed, and the flowing Spirit regenerates.

We have seen that the Trinity has consummated Himself to the uttermost in this consummation—the New Jerusalem. This picture shows us much more than what is recorded in the New Testament. The New Testament gives us a longer record, but what is recorded there is not as bountiful as it is consummated here in the ultimate consummation. What is here is not just a sketch or an extract but a development. Without this ultimate consummation it would be hard for us to realize that in the New Testament the Trinity is five-fold for our entrance, our constitution, our living, our enjoyment, which is fellowship, feeding, and satisfaction, and for our existence for us to participate in the Creator, in the Redeemer, and in the Regenerator. Without such a view I do not think we would be able to realize that in the New Testament the Triune God is so much to us. Such a five-fold Triune God is the temple to us (Rev. 21:22). He is our eternal abode in which we will dwell forever. Our eternal abode, our "heavenly mansion," will not be common or ordinary but very particular, very special. It will be an extraordinary dwelling place, not an ordinary dwelling place people can live in. Only the particular, extraordinary people with a high rank have the right to live in the temple. Who are these particular, high ranked people? They are the sons of God. Revelation 21:7 indicates that the sons of God will inherit this. Now we can see how much the Triune God has been consummated in this ultimate consummation. You young brothers need to be diligent to get into these things. You should not follow the tradition and remain under its influence. You have read Revelation 21 and 22 again and again in a superficial way, which is the general practice of many Christians. You need to spend more time to dig into it. These points I have shared with you did not come to me by accident. I have studied these two chapters for many, many years.

USING THESE POINTS FOR GOSPEL PREACHING

If we would present all these rich points in our messages to the saints, I do believe we could use all these points for preaching the gospel. We can preach the gospel with all these items to the sinners to show them what the ultimate consummation of God's salvation is. We can show them that the ultimate consummation of God's salvation is to enjoy God in His Trinity in such a wonderful, excellent, bountiful, and marvelous way. Do not think that the sinners cannot understand. With the proper presentation I believe they can understand. We must point out all the blessings. The temple as our particular, peculiar, high ranked dwelling place is God Himself. Every item is a person, not a matter or a thing but the Person of the Triune God. You must tell them what kind of Triune God we have. Such a Triune God eventually will be our high ranked dwelling place in eternity forever. A Person is our dwelling place. He Himself is the city, the house. He is also the light, the tree, and the river. All these items are the Triune Person, the Triune God. Even the street we walk on is the divine Person. The three-fold person is our street, our bread, and our drink. This is marvelous. He is our way, He is our living, He is our food, and He is our drink. Then you can tell the listening sinners that they can enjoy this right now. This person is their Creator, God; He is their Redeemer, the Lamb; and He is their Regenerator, the living water. You must tell them that right away they can enjoy God as their Creator, the Lamb as their Redeemer, and the living water, the Spirit, as their Regenerator. They will be regenerated and their regeneration will be the entrance into this wonderful, bountiful, marvelous enjoyment. I believe the sinners will be able to understand. It all depends in what way we present these matters. There is the need of our "cooking." If we cook these matters, we can preach the very best gospel from the New Jerusalem. Do not think I have finished the consummation. Actually, more messages are needed to finish this consummation. I have just given you a small taste.

HEBREWS 11

After hearing this, some dissenters who have some biblical knowledge in a traditional way may refer you to Hebrews 11. He may read you verses 9 and 10 which tell us, "By faith he [Abraham] dwelt as a foreigner in the land of promise as in a land not his own, dwelling in tents with Isaac and Jacob, the joint heirs of the same promise; for he waited for the city which has the foundations, whose Architect and Maker is God." The dissenters would argue that Abraham was waiting for a city, considering himself to have no land and no place. He was waiting for a city built by God as the Architect and as the Maker. This city must be a real city. Then they may quote verse 14 which says, "For those who say such things show clearly that they seek a country of their own." At this point you must ask them what the country is. Is it Palestine? He would surely say that the country is heaven. If he says this he has lost his case already because you can tell him that the

New Jerusalem will come down out of heaven (Rev. 21:10). The New Jerusalem which they think is a physical city will leave the country which Abraham waited for. Abraham was seeking a country they treasure, but eventually the very "heavenly mansion" will come down from that country, leaving that country in the heavens.

They might also read verses 15 and 16 which say, "And if indeed they had been remembering that country from which they went out, they would have had opportunity to return; but now they longed after a better country, that is, a heavenly one." To them heaven is the better country. But we must keep in mind that this verse does not say a country in the heavens but a heavenly country. An American in America has a different denotation than an American man. The rest of verse 16 says, "Wherefore God is not ashamed of them to be called upon as their God, for He has prepared for them a city." They might then ask you, "Is not this city the New Jerusalem?" Their understanding in their natural mentality is that the New Jerusalem will be a physical, material city. But brothers, we must be very conversant with the spiritual understanding of such an item in the Bible.

The Triune God made a plan in eternity past. He has been carrying out an economy throughout all the centuries. The Son came through incarnation, lived on this earth for thirty-three and a half years, died on the cross, and was resurrected and ascended. Then the Spirit came and worked out many wonderful things. Eventually, do you believe that as a conclusion God would merely build a physical city for His redeemed people to live in? This is too low. The New Jerusalem is a city, but what kind of city is it? Is it a physical, material city? Some might say that it is such a city of gold, pearls, and precious stones. When they say this we must refer them to 1 Corinthians 3. Paul said that he had laid the unique foundation and he charged us to be careful how we build upon it. We should build with gold, silver, and precious stones to build the church. Then we need to ask them if we build the church today with real gold, silver, and precious stones. Surely they would say that Paul was not referring to real gold, silver, and precious stones. We must then tell them that the New Jerusalem should be interpreted in the same way and that the New Jerusalem is the consummation of the building in 1 Corinthians 3. In 1 Corinthians 3 the building is in the process and has not yet been consummated. The New Jerusalem is the consummation of that building. Abraham was waiting for a city, not a material city, but a marvelous city built with the Father's nature, with the Son's redemption, and with the Spirit's transformation. This fellowship may help us see this vision and after seeing this vision how to help others.

THE ETERNAL GOD—OUR DWELLING PLACE

You could also tell them that our God expects not only to be our Creator, our Redeemer, our life, our life supply, our wisdom, righteousness, sanctification, redemption, but He also expects to be our dwelling place. Actually, this New Jerusalem is the processed God expanded into eternity for you and I to live in. Perhaps someone new would ask how God could be our dwelling place. We should answer by referring him to Deuteronomy 33:27 which says the eternal God is our dwelling place (American Standard Version). He is a strong dwelling place to preserve you from trouble. As our dwelling place He is our refuge. Psalm 90 which is a psalm of Moses, the man of God, tells us, "Lord, thou hast been our dwelling place in all generations" (v. 1). Then you could read Psalm 27:4 which says, "One [thing] have I asked of Jehovah, that will I seek after: that I may dwell in the house of Jehovah all the days of my life, to behold the beauty of Jehovah, and to inquire [of him] in his temple" (Darby's New Translation). David had a desire to dwell in the temple all the time, not just for one hour, one morning, or one evening, but all the time to behold the Lord's beauty. Even the Old Testament saints considered God as their dwelling place and they desired to dwell in this place to behold God all the time. Then what about the New Testament believers, all the redeemed ones in eternity? Shall they live in a physical, golden city with physical pearls and physical stones? We must say no to this. They will live in God Himself. The eternal God will be their eternal dwelling place. He will be the particular dwelling place, the temple, in which we will dwell.

If we would get ourselves into this matter, then we would be able to preach, teach, and present this matter to anyone. They would have no way to debate with us. We must not take care of this carelessly, but with our full spiritual energy. Dear saints, we must study this. The last two chapters of the entire Bible are really worthwhile of our study for years. This leaven of the heavenly mansion must be purged away.

We all can see now how much the traditional teachings, concepts, understanding, and influence have held us back from the deeper study of the pure Word. We read Revelation 21 and 22 many times but we just took it for granted. We never had any thought to dig into it or to study it further. We must leave the tradition behind and go further to study. We must be like Columbus who left tradition to sail on and on. Eventually he reached a new land. We have to sail on. Year after year there should be new material—every page of the book of Revelation can be used as material for gospel preaching.

THREE CATEGORIES OF PEOPLE

You could preach the gospel using the three categories of people in Revelation 21:3-8. The best category of people is the sons of God. The worst category of people are those in the lake of fire and the middle category of people are those who are neither in the New Jerusalem nor in the lake of fire but outside of the city. The sons are in the city drinking the river of life, eating the tree of life, and walking in the light of life. Those in the lake of fire just suffer the burning. The middle class of people do not suffer the burning, nor do they enjoy the tree of life, the river of life, or the light of life. They only eat the leaves of the tree and they do not walk in the light directly but outside the city. Many Christians are not clear about these three categories of people in Revelation 21 and 22. In their general concept there will be only two categories of people, the saved ones and the perished ones, in eternity.

THE BLESSING OF THE ETERNAL LIFE VERSUS THE BLESSING TO THE PEOPLES ON THE NEW EARTH

Even the last hymn in our hymnal, 1348, is a wrong hymn based upon our present realization. This hymn is comprised of Revelation 21:3-4 which says, "And I heard a loud voice out of the throne, saying, Behold, the tabernacle of God is with men, and He shall tabernacle with them, and they shall be His peoples, and God Himself shall be with them. And He shall wipe away every tear from their eyes; and death shall be no more; nor sorrow, nor crying, nor pain—they shall be no more; for the former things have passed away." The only problem with this hymn is that this word was not spoken to the believers but to the peoples on the new earth outside the holy city. When we sang this hymn were we singing it to the people outside the city? I do not believe this hymn was written with this understanding. This really troubles me that this hymn was written and placed in our hymnal. Our Recovery Version of Revelation titles verse 3 and 4 of chapter 21 as "Peoples on the New Earth." Verses 5 through 7 are titled "Sons of God in Eternity." Verses 3 and 4 were spoken to the unbelievers who are the descendants of the sheep in Matthew 25:31-46. Verses 5 through 7 refer to the sons of God, all the saints, the divinely saved ones through the generations. Hymn 1348 says nothing about the inheritance. It says nothing about the tree of life, the river of water of life, or the light of life. This hymn says that "God shall wipe away all tears from their eyes" (21:4). When we believers are there in the

New Jerusalem there is no possibility of tears. In our vocabulary there will not be such a word. But the dictionary outside the city still will have this word. That means they will still have tears. If they did not have tears they would not need someone to wipe them away. I do not think that anyone of us who sang this hymn in the past discerned that this was a wrong hymn. This is because we never got into the real blessing of the eternal life in the New Jerusalem. For God to wipe away tears with no sorrow or crying or pain are the blessings outside the city without eternal life. These are the blessings rendered to the unbelieving, God-created and restored people. These are the nations, not the sons of God. We are the sons of God. Because we are still the old creation, we still have tears. But when we get into the New Jerusalem we will no longer be the old creation and there will be no tears. The restored nations, however, are still in the old creation. They still will have tears. The blessings to them will be that God will wipe away their tears. You may think this is an intimate blessing and that if God would wipe away your tears this would be marvelous. This indicates that you have never gotten into the blessing of the eternal life. The blessing of the eternal life is not to wipe away your tears but to fill you with another kind of water. If you are filled within with the living water, tears would never come out.

We have received the eternal life, yet many of us did not know what the real blessing of this life was and what the real blessing of this eternal life would be in eternity, in the New Jerusalem. If you want God to wipe away your tears, there will be no tears in the New Jerusalem. In the next edition of the hymnal we will replace this hymn with a positive one about the blessings of the eternal life in which the sons of God will participate.

THE NEED TO KNOW THE INTRINSIC ESSENCE OF LIFE IN THE LORD'S RECOVERY

The fact that this hymn made it into our supplement

shows that with just a little carelessness something is able to creep in. This is why I felt an urgent need to call this gathering with all of you, and this is why I opened up the door to embrace so many young ones who are not elders. I do have a burden to present to you what the Lord has shown us in all these years. This might be considered a constitution, just as the constitution has controlled the United States for two hundred years. We do need a controlling constitution that will rule out many things such as hymn 1348. I do believe that the brother who wrote this hymn wrote it with a very good intention. The intention was very positive, yet the work was terrible. This shows us that in our preaching and in our teaching we may have already done things like this unconsciously. We do not realize that some damage has been caused already by our so-called ministry. However, we still think our ministry is wonderful, just as the writer of hymn 1348 thought his writing was wonderful. Some teachings have gone out in the same principle. They were not in the intrinsic essence of the Lord's vision in His recovery. No damage has been done yet, but the principle of life has been changed and eventually "the mustard seed" will not grow into an herb but into a big tree. It will not be an herb for feeding people but a big tree for lodging evil things and evil persons.

This is why I was burdened to have such a gathering to make all the crucial items of the Lord's recovery so clear to all of us. We must be on the alert. We should not merely take care of others, but we must take care of ourselves. We should not think that we are okay and that we are safeguarded. We all must take heed to our own preaching, our own teaching, our own so-called ministry. We must ask whether the principle of life has been changed or not. We must know the intrinsic essence of life in the Lord's recovery.

CHAPTER SEVEN

THE VISION CONCERNING THE NEW JERUSALEM— THE ULTIMATE CONSUMMATION

(3)

The ultimate consummation, the New Jerusalem, is the consummation of the entire divine revelation, the Bible, and of all the wonderful items contained in the Bible as the complete revelation of God. How much you can get into the items of the ultimate consummation depends upon your knowledge of the truth, your ability, and your degree of endeavoring in the truth.

THE TRIUNE GOD AS THE CONSTITUTION OF THE NEW JERUSALEM

We have seen that one of the aspects of the Trinity contained in this ultimate consummation is that the Triune God Himself comprises the basic elements for the building up and the constitution of the New Jerusalem as the gold, pearls, and precious stones.

The Gold

We can easily understand that gold refers to the Father's nature. We must see that the gold in the New Jerusalem is a consummation of all the items of gold used as figures in both the Old and New Testaments beginning from Genesis 2. At the flow of the river in Genesis 2 there is gold (vv. 10-12). In the book of Exodus, gold was used extensively in the building of the tabernacle. Also, in the book of Zechariah is a golden lampstand (4:2). There are two golden pipes and golden oil (4:12). Then in the New Testament Paul tells us that he laid the unique foundation and that this foundation needs to be built upon with gold, silver, and precious stones (1 Cor. 3:10-12). Peter also said that the proving of our faith is much more precious than that of gold (1 Pet. 1:7). In addition, the Lord charged the church in Laodicea to buy from Him gold refined by fire that they might be rich (Rev. 3:18). These are just some of the verses we need to study in order to see the significance of the consummation of gold in the New Jerusalem.

Many of you young brothers have consecrated yourselves to the Lord with your whole life, not only your whole time. You must consider what you must do. To serve the Lord with your full time and with your whole life does not mean you need to do much work. You must realize that to serve the Lord is not to do a work nor is it to carry out a big Christian career. To serve the Lord is to minister the Lord, the Triune God, as everything from within the revelation of the holy Word with all the basic truths. This is the main thing. This is your capital. If you know more basic truths from the Bible, you have more capital. If you do not have any truth, you are a poor one with an empty hand to serve the Lord. Whenever I come to this point my heart is broken and my spirit is burning for you. According to my observation you have not done the best job in acquiring these basic truths. Even if you are still under the age of sixty you can still do a lot of studying. Even at the age of eighty I must testify that I study the Bible every day. How could we serve the Lord without the capital of the adequate knowledge and experience of the divine truths? I am very much burdened for you all in this matter.

We have just finished the Life-study of the entire New Testament and most of these messages have been published. There are many pages filled with many points of the truth for us to study. When we are ministering the Word in the meeting it is not sufficient merely to go to the pages of the Life-study to pick up a subject and to pick up some points without much study. This does not work. Even to give one message in one meeting you need the capital.

You must study the gold in the Bible from Genesis 2 through Revelation 21 to fully understand the gold in its ultimate consummation. Go to the Strong's Concordance and take down all the verses with the word gold or golden used. Then spend a month to study these verses, to study the gold. See what is there in the divine revelation. This is the way to get the capital. After such a study you would begin to see something. You would see the gold as the base of the mountain on which the New Jerusalem is built. It is its base, its sight, and its ground. The city proper is like a mountain with a height of twelve thousand stadia and the city is pure gold, like pure glass (Rev. 21:16-18). After such study then you would know the ultimate consummation of the significance of gold used as a divine figure in the Bible.

As we have seen, gold in the New Jerusalem signifies the Father's nature. Gold is a sign of the nature of God the Father, not a sign of work or doing. Gold is a matter of essence and nature. It is a substance which no one can improve and which no one can produce. Please do not think that I have exhausted everything of the spiritual, divine, heavenly, and holy significances of all the items in the Bible. I cannot do that and I am not that all-inclusive. What I am doing is to open up the mines for you to go in and dig. Even in these messages I have spoken quite a number of points which were not covered in the Life-study messages. I have also seen more in the last eight years concerning the New Jerusalem since I wrote the notes to the Recovery Version of Revelation in 1976. This again shows us that we must get into the depths of all the truths in the Bible.

Pearl

Pearl signifies Christ's Person in His redemptive death and life-secreting resurrection (Rev. 21:21). Pearl is produced of an oyster. When the oyster gets wounded by a particle of sand it secretes its life-juice around the sand, making it a pearl. Such a produce denotes Christ the Person in His redemptive death and life-secreting resurrection.

Precious Stones

Then we come to the jasper stone of the wall and the twelve precious stones of the foundation. Some of us must study the twelve different kinds of precious stones in the New Jerusalem (Rev. 21:14, 19-20). You need to study the best lexicons and the experts' study of these kinds of minerals. I believe there is much spiritual significance in all these different stones. (The Lord may lead us to have a special training on the book of Revelation after we have finished the entire New Testament. We need at least thirty more messages on this book). God's Word does not have any word of waste. Even a small preposition bears a lot of meaning. These twelve stones as the wall and the foundation of this ultimate consummation must bear a great significance. I did have a burden to study these twelve stones, but I did not have the time. Many of you young brothers should pick up the burden to spend a year's time, even more, just to study the twelve precious stones of the New Jerusalem. This is worthwhile.

This is why I told some of you already that I do not like you to put the Life-studies aside with the footnotes in the Recovery Version. Our fellowship in the last chapter concerning the inclusion of hymn 1348 in our hymnal gives me the ground to say this. The outline in the Recovery Version for chapter twenty-one of Revelation clearly titles verses 3 through 4 "Peoples on the New Earth" and verses 5 through 7 "Sons of God in Eternity." I made this so clear in the Recovery Version, yet still this hymn slipped into our hymnal. This means that if the editors of this hymnal and even the ones who arranged the numbers for the hymnal had picked up the proper knowledge from the notes of Revelation, they should have discerned that this was a wrong hymn. I never really looked into the supplement until one day a few months ago, and then I saw this hymn. This shows that many of you have passed through the trainings, but you missed much of the basic truths. The dear ones who edited and arranged this supplement have been with us many years, but the inclusion of this hymn indicates that they did not get into the depths of the book of Revelation. Still, some of you like to put the Life-studies and the Recovery Versions aside and go to the other books. I am not belittling others' books, but I would ask you what better things you could get there. The better and more basic things are in the Recovery Versions and the Life-study messages, but because this is your property you do not treasure it. Most of what the Lord has shown us in these past years has been printed. I feel sorry that so much of Brother Nee's ministry has not yet been put into print. This is why I had the burden to put all the things that the Lord has shown us into print. All these truths are in print and they are worthwhile of your study for five to ten years.

When standing on the shoulders of these truths you can go further to study the twelve precious stones. I hope that maybe six or eight young brothers would spend one year to study these twelve stones. I believe you can do a complete job within one year, since this is a big job. In addition to studying by using the lexicons and other Bible-study helps, it would help to get the stones themselves. Precious stones signify the transforming work of the Spirit with all the divine elements. Transforming work needs elements. A piece of wood can be petrified by being replaced with all the mineral elements. The Spirit, which is the flowing water, flows with divine elements to transform our entire being. Since this book of Revelation is made known to us by signs, all the precious stones are signs signifying the Spirit's transforming work with all the divine elements carried and constituted into our being to transform us from clay pieces into precious stones. It is worthwhile to study these signs.

This is the Trinity as the constitution of this ultimate consummation—the Father's nature, the Son as the precious One in His redemptive death and in His life-imparting resurrection, and the Spirit as the flow in His transforming work with all the divine elements. This is the ultimate consummation of the Trinity in one of His aspects. There are many more things to say concerning the book of Revelation, and we may need an entire year with two trainings to do an adequate job. The golden lampstands in chapter one and the ultimate consummation of the New Jerusalem in chapters twenty-one and twenty-two still need more ministry.

CHAPTERS SIX THROUGH TWENTY OF REVELATION

Chapters six through twenty of Revelation are actually a parenthetical section because Revelation is a book on the church. The focus of the Bible is not the world situation. The focus of the Bible is Christ and the church. The first three chapters of Revelation are on the church, chapters four and five are on Christ, and the last two chapters are on the consummation of the church. Chapters six trough twenty, though, are a section of God's governmental, universal administration to purify and clear up the entire universe by judging and eliminating all the negative things. The last enemy, death, will be dealt with along with Satan, who held it as might and who is cast into the lake of fire. After this, the entire universe is cleared up and becomes a new universe, a new heaven and a new earth. Revelation six through twenty is, therefore, a section on God's universal government to deal with His enemy and all the negative things.

Within this parenthetical section, the church and the saints are referred to seventeen times:

1) In 6:9-11 the martyred souls who are still under the altar cried to the Lord. The cry of the martyred souls constitutes the fifth seal in Revelation and ushers in

the sixth seal, which is the initial step of the great tribulation.

2) In 7:9-17 is an innumerable multitude under the Lamb's overshadowing care. While the judgment of all the calamities is taking place, Christ will overshadow His redeemed ones.

3) In 8:3-5 Christ is the High Priest offering all the suffering saints' prayer, with His incense added, to God. God's answer to this prayer is to judge the rebellious world.

4) 11:18 mentions the reward given to the Lord's slaves, the prophets, the saints, and those who fear His name. This reward will be given by the Lord to His faithful ones at His coming back.

5) In 12:1-17 is the universal woman with the man-child. It is the man-child that causes the great dragon to be cast down from the heavens to the earth.

6) In 13:7 the beast, the Antichrist, was allowed to war with the saints and to overcome them.

7) The firstfruit of the believers before the great tribulation, the one hundred and forty-four thousand, is in 14:1-5.

8) In 14:13 are the martyred saints in the great tribulation and their blessing.

9) In 14:14-16 is the harvest of believers near the end of the great tribulation.

10) In 15:2-4 are the martyrs who had been under Antichrist's persecution standing upon the glassy sea.

11) During the tribulation there is a warning given to the remaining saints to keep their garments in 16:15.

12) In 17:14 are those saints who were called and chosen

and faithful. They were selected to be an army to fight Antichrist and the false prophet.

13) In 18:4 the Lord calls His children, "Come out of her, My people." To come out out of her means to come out of both religious Babylon and material Babylon since Babylon the Great is twofold.

14) In 19:7-9 is the Bride ready for Christ's wedding.

15) Revelation 19:14 mentions the heavenly armies composed of the overcomers who will be the ready Bride.

16) In 20:4 and 6 we see the co-kings of Christ in the manifestation of the kingdom of the heavens.

17) Then the camp of the saints surrounded by the rebellious nations instigated by Satan is in 20:9.

These seventeen instances of the church in this parenthetical section need much study. If we would study these instances we would see something and have something new, solid, and basic to minister to the churches. This kind of study and ministry would encourage me. If we would study these instances, we would understand much more concerning God's economy related to the church and the saints. These seventeen instances are inserted into this parenthetical section. During this time, God will be carrying out His universal, governmental administration.

THE NEED OF MUCH STUDY

You young brothers are in a golden time because you have many years to study these precious things if the Lord delays His coming. I believe that all this wonderful knowledge will be very useful in the millennium and in eternity. If you do not pick this knowledge up today it will be too late. You will be the "later graduates."

The Ultimate Consummation of the Stones

Again let me emphasize that we must study the consummation of all the stones in the Bible from Genesis 2. Onyx is the very first stone mentioned in the Bible and one of the last stones mentioned in the Bible is jasper. This is very interesting and needs your study. You also must study the twelve stones on the breastplate of Urim and Thummim and the stones on the shoulders of the high priest. By such study you will receive something.

When you present these things to the saints, even the new ones among us will enjoy hearing them. You will attract people, and the church will be built up through the saints being edified by you. Then your preaching or teaching will enrich the ministry in the Lord's recovery. You do not need to go to the traditional teachings in the books on your shelves. Many marvelous mines in the twenty-seven books of the New Testament have been opened up in these last ten years. The only problem is that we did not take the time to dig in them. Do not go away from these mines to other sources, hoping to get something there. You must see the ultimate consummation of all the stones.

The Ultimate Consummation of the River

Then you must go on to study and see the ultimate consummation of the river with the water of life in the Bible. In Genesis 2 we see a river flowing out of Eden to water the garden that parts into four heads (v. 10). In Exodus there is the flowing water out of the cleft rock. Psalm 46 tells us that there is a river whose streams make glad the city of God (v. 4), and Psalm 36:8 tells us that the Lord will make us to drink of the river of His pleasures. Also, in Ezekiel 47 we see a river that brings life wherever it goes (v. 9). Finally, in Revelation 22:1 we see a river of water of life proceeding out of the throne of God and of the Lamb. In the book of Revelation there are some minor things which should not be considered as consummations of the things in the other books of the Bible. But all the major things are the consummation of items already existing in the Bible. This is because Revelation is a book of the harvest of all the truths in the Bible. It is the harvest of all the seeds of the divine truth which have been sown and grown up throughout the Scriptures. This is why in Ezekiel 47 the water is issuing out of God's house (vv. 1-2), which nearly matches Revelation 22 with the water proceeding out of the throne of God. From God's temple there is water flowing and from God's throne there is water flowing. Then in the New Testament the Lord Jesus says that if we drink of Him we will have rivers of living water flowing out of our innermost being (John 7:37-38). Paul also tells us that the Israelites in the wilderness drank the same spiritual drink and that they drank of Christ who was the spiritual rock which followed them (1 Cor. 10:4). In Revelation chapter seven we see that the Lamb shepherds the saints and guides them to springs of waters of life (v. 17). In 21:6 it says that God will give to the thirsty one from the spring of the water of life freely. Also, in chapter twenty-two is the ultimate calling in the entire Bible. The Spirit and the Bride say that whosoever is thirsty must come to drink the water of life (v. 17). This needs much study. This is the consummation of the river and of the water of life in the Bible.

The Ultimate Consummation of Light and Life

We also need to study light throughout the Bible with its consummation. We have to go to all the references of light in the Old Testament and in the New Testament. In Genesis 1 are the fourth day lights. Psalm 36 says, "In thy light shall we see light" (v. 9). Isaiah 2:5 says, "O house of Jacob, come ye, and let us walk in the light of the Lord." Peter tells us that we have been called out of darkness into His marvelous light (1 Pet. 2:9). Even Paul was charged by the Lord to preach the gospel to open peoples' eyes and to turn them from darkness to light (Acts 26:18). There are many references to light in the Old and New Testaments which we must study. Once you have studied light throughout the Bible, then you can see that the light in Revelation 21 is a consummation of all the light in the Bible. We have also seen that the tree of life, the river of life, and the light of life are the consummation of the divine life throughout the Bible. This also needs our study.

THE FIVE-FOLD TRINITY
IN THE ULTIMATE CONSUMMATION

In this ultimate consummation we must also see that the Trinity is the entrance. The three gates on each side (Rev. 21:13) signify the entrance through the Triune God. Luke 15 shows us this three-fold entrance. The Son came to redeem (v. 4), the Spirit came to seek and find the lost one and to bring him back to the Father (v. 8), and lastly the Father receives the lost one back to Himself (v. 20). The Son's redeeming, the Spirit's seeking, and the Father's receiving are a complete entrance into the New Jerusalem. We can also see these three gates in 1 Peter 1:2. We were selected according to the foreknowledge of God the Father. God the Father's selection is the initiation; God the Spirit's sanctification carries out the selection of God the Father; and God the Son's redemption, signified by His sprinkled blood, is the completion. This again is the three gates of the Trinity. Another reference to the Triune God being our entrance into the holy city is Ephesians 2:18 which says, "For through Him we both have access in one Spirit unto the Father." The second point of the Trinity in the New Jerusalem is that the Trinity is the intrinsic element as the gold, the pearl, and the precious stones for the building up and the constitution of this ultimate consummation. Third, the Trinity in this ultimate consummation is for the living of God's redeemed ones. They walk on the golden street, feed on the tree of life, and drink of the water of life. Fourth, the Trinity is also for their enjoyment. To enjoy the

Triune God is to be enlightened, to be fed, and to be satisfied. God the Father is the light of life, God the Son is the tree of life, and God the Spirit is the water of life for the enjoyment of His chosen and redeemed people. Finally, a more basic item of the Trinity in the New Jerusalem is that He is God our Creator, the Lamb our Redeemer, and the Spirit as the river of the water of life, our Regenerator. As a human being you need to pass through these three steps: created, redeemed, and regenerated. We can at least see these five aspects of the divine Trinity in the New Jerusalem. The divine Trinity is for our being, the divine Trinity is for our entry into this ultimate consummation, the divine Trinity is for the building up, the constitution of such an ultimate consummation, and finally, the divine Trinity is for our living and for our enjoyment.

Second Corinthians 13:14 also shows us something concerning the enjoyment of the divine Trinity: "The grace of the Lord Jesus Christ, and the love of God, and the fellowship of the Holy Spirit be with you all." The fellowship of the Spirit is the flow of the river. The grace of Christ is the tree of life for our supply, and the love of God is just like the light of God. Love is the nature of God's essence. Light is the nature of God's expression. Both love and light are the nature of what God is.

SPIRIT, LIFE, LOVE, AND LIGHT

The New Testament tells us four main things concerning what God is: God is Spirit (John 4:24), God is life (John 1:4; 10:10; 14:6), God is love (1 John 4:8, 16), and God is light (1 John 1:5). These four items are fully covered in the notes of the Recovery Version of the Epistles of John. I am concerned that some of you were in the training on these Epistles, but you still do not know what the Spirit, love, light, and life are. Let us read part of note 5[3] in 1 John chapter 1 to see what these terms mean:

"Such an expression, like God is love in 4:8, 16,

and God is Spirit in John 4:24, is used not in a metaphoric sense but in a predicative sense. They denote and describe the nature of God. In His nature God is Spirit, love, and light. Spirit denotes the nature of God's Person; love, the nature of God's essence; and light, the nature of God's expression. Both love and light are related to God as life, which life is of the Spirit (Rom. 8:2). God, Spirit, and life are actually one. God is Spirit, and Spirit is life. Within such a life are love and light. When this divine love appears to us, it becomes grace, and when this divine light shines upon us, it becomes truth."

These terms are clearly defined and covered in this note but many of you never got into it. Therefore, this has not become your capital in your ministry. You do not have this basic realization within your being. Then when you minister the Word to God's people you do not have the rich capital. As a result, you are short of feelings, short of thoughts, short of words, short of points, and short of expression. Thus, your speaking is poor without anything interesting to people. But if you are equipped and enriched within your being you know that the Spirit denotes the nature of God's Person in John 4:24, love denotes the nature of God's essence, and that light denotes the nature of God's expression. God's life is also carried by God's Spirit and within this life are love and light. This is clear and this is rich. You must be saturated with this kind of knowledge. You should soak yourself in these things. If you would stay in this note for one day, you would never forget it. I am concerned that such a note is here in the Recovery Version, yet you would disregard it and go to other books.

This kind of knowledge is not merely objective. The more you would read this note the more you would be nourished. Then when you minister to people they would receive some nourishment. We could preach four or five messages out of this one note for our gospel preaching, telling people that our God is not like the idols. The nature of our God's Person is Spirit. This provides good material for gospel preaching. Many of us preach from the traditional concept that God loves the world and that the sinners are going to hell. It is true that God loves us but there is nothing fresh, nothing new and nothing interesting in this for people. We can tell people how God in nature is Spirit, and how God who is Spirit in nature is also love. You not only tell people that God loves them but you also need to tell them that God is love, which is the nature of His essence. Then you need to tell them that God is light in His expression, and this God who is light is also life.

The entire Bible is the gospel and especially the book of Romans in its entirety is the gospel. However, we have never been taught, educated, or raised up in this way. We have neither been saturated in or equipped with all these divine truths. These things have not become a part of our being. Our entire being needs to be reconstituted with all these things until they become our constituent. Then our preaching will be very much strengthened and enriched. We will preach something intrinsically essential and we will be teaching the basic revelation in the Holy Scriptures. This is the New Testament ministry. Do not go to study the so-called theology. That is too superficial. Hardly any of these teachings get into the intrinsic nature of the divine Person and His divine work. The New Testament ministry is absolutely different from this. The vision that the Lord has given us in His recovery is following the New Testament ministry; it is not following traditional theology. Many people with a Ph.D. in theology would not be able to tell you what it means to say that God is Spirit, God is love, God is light, and God is life. This is why I strongly urge you not to leave the "diamonds" the Lord has given to us on your bookshelf and spend your time on other writings. To spend your money and time in other books is a waste when you compare this with spending your time on the precious things the Lord has shown us which are there in the notes of the Recovery Version and in the Life-study messages.

A WORD OF LOVE

Please do not consider my word as a rebuke or as a warning. I hope you realize that my word is a word of love. I love the churches, I love all the saints, and I love you all. I do not like to see your time, money, and energy wasted. To teach and to preach things other than the New Testament ministry itself delays people and to some extent it holds them back, distracts them, and misleads them. I do not like to see this. My heart is broken. I like to see you redeem your time, save your energy, and save your money so that you may save others' time. One message which is not in the central lane of the New Testament ministry wastes a lot of energy and a lot of time for the saints. They must listen to you and they must read your writings. This could waste their time and maybe mislead and distract them. At least it holds them back. This is why I was so burdened to call this urgent gathering. We must stop any kind of traditional ministry. We must come back to the unique New Testament ministry which the Lord has shown us in the past sixty years. This has become our vision. This is a word of love. I have no intention to rebuke you, to discredit you, or to condemn you. I do not even have the intention to warn you. That is not my business and that is not my heart. My heart is just that I love you brothers. You have consecrated your entire future to take this way. Why do you need to waste your time and thus waste others' time? Others must listen to you and read your materials and they get the wrong impression. You must consider how to save the saints' time. Do not give them anything that will hold them back. We must consider what we speak in the meetings and what we write and publish in print. We must consider whether this material would take the saints on speedily or would hold them back, distract them, or mislead them. We are not living in Martin Luther's time. We are living at the end of the twentieth century and the Lord's recovery has passed through so many centuries already. In these last sixty years the Lord has shown us many things and we have done our best to put these into print. These things should not remain on your bookshelves while you go back to the old writings. This is not wise. My love would not allow me to be silent. This is why we are here. I hope that all of you would accept this word and drop the old things and go forward.

CHAPTER EIGHT

THE VISION CONCERNING THE NEW JERUSALEM— THE ULTIMATE CONSUMMATION

(4)

A COMPOSITION OF LIVING PERSONS

A Pillar in the Temple

Revelation 3:12 says, "He who overcomes, I will make him a pillar in the temple of My God, and he shall by no means go out anymore, and I will write upon him the name of My God and the name of the city of My God, the New Jerusalem, which descends out of heaven from My God, and My new name." The point in this verse is crucial—in the coming temple of God, the pillar is a person. He who overcomes will be made a pillar in the temple of God. We have seen already in 21:22 that John told us he saw no temple in the New Jerusalem because its temple is the Lord God the Almighty and the Lamb. The temple is also a person; it is not a physical matter. If a pillar in the temple is a person and the temple itself is a Person, do you believe the New Jerusalem is a physical city composed of physical stones, physical pearls, and physical gold? Could it be that the pillar is a person, the temple is a Person, but not the city? To interpret the city as something physical is not logical.

Living Stones

The New Jerusalem, as we have seen, is the consummation of all the building in the Bible. In the Old

Testament the tabernacle and the temple are typified by physical matters. In the Old Testament there is physical gold in the tabernacle and there are real precious stones on the breastplate and shoulder-pieces of the priest. But when we come to the fulfillment of God's building in the New Testament, there is nothing merely physical. The stones in God's building are living persons. When Peter came to the Lord the first time, He called him Cephas, which means a stone (John 1:42). Peter later wrote in his first Epistle that the Lord Himself is a living stone and that we believers are also living stones (2:4-5). Paul also told us that as a wise master builder he had laid the foundation of God's building upon which we, the believers, should build with gold, silver, and precious stones (1 Cor. 3:10-12). Surely the stones are not physical things. These are persons, which are confirmed by Peter's writing that all of the believers are living stones. The holy city, therefore, as the consummation of God's building in the Bible, is not something physical but personal. The entire city is personal, not physical. This interpretation is fully logical.

A Physical Building versus a Personal Building

We must also ask ourselves whether or not, in the entire universe, God has a physical building and He is also now building a personal building. According to the traditional teaching in John 14, the Lord has gone back to the heavens to build a physical, heavenly mansion. This means that today the Lord in His heavenly ministry is building a physical building in the heavens and a spiritual building on earth. He is now building a physical building with real stones, pearls, and much gold, and at the same time on this earth He is building a personal temple.

If there is a physical city at the end of the Bible, though, we must ask where the spiritual building built by the Lord is. If there is a material temple in the heavens and a spiritual one on earth, where is the spiritual building when the physical one comes down out of heaven? The only way to interpret this is that the spiritual one merges into the physical one. As we can see, this interpretation is entirely illogical. Can we really believe that the Lord today is building two houses? A strange point about this kind of interpretation is that the physical building is in the heavens and the spiritual building is on the earth. On the earth He is building a spiritual house and in the heavens He is building a physical one. Consider what the Lord would have to do to build such a physical building. He would have to collect many pearls and the pearls would have to be very big, at least eight feet in diameter, in order to be a gate through which people could pass. If the pearls were that big consider how big the oyster would have to be to produce such pearls. Pearls are not created, but produced by the living oyster. Also, could we believe that there would be a literal mountain of gold more than thirteen hundred miles high? Some may say that God is universally great and that He can build such a mountain. However, if God could build such a mountain, why would He need two thousand years in which to build it?

The word given in John 14, which some people interpret as the Lord going to prepare "a heavenly mansion," was spoken two thousand years ago. This interpretation tells us that the Lord went to the heavens to prepare such a mansion and that when He comes back He will receive us to Himself there. According to this interpretation He has not finished the building there in the heavens. He is still there building the heavenly mansion. This, however, is against the principle of God's creation. In God's creation, God speaks things into being. He says there is light and light is there. When God says there is gold, gold is there. In God's creation, He speaks not being as being (Rom. 4:17). Since such is the principle in God's creation, why has it taken nearly two thousand years to build such a big physical house in the heavens? Also, why would such a big physical building need to come down to earth? Why would the Lord not call not being into being on the earth? Again, we have to say that this interpretation is not logical. To say that the Lord is now building a physical building in the heavens and that when He comes that physical building will come down from the heavens is an improper understanding of the Bible.

We have seen that according to the book of Revelation itself this building is undoubtedly personal, not physical, because the temple is God and the Lamb Himself, and the pillar is an overcomer. These are strong proofs that the city is not physical but a composition of living persons. This is also fully confirmed by the New Testament revelation. In the New Testament a believer in Christ is considered a piece of stone like Peter. Then in the Epistles, the apostles considered the believers as pieces of living and precious stones. I do not believe that the Lord would spend two thousand years to build up something and then eventually put this building aside or merge this building with a physical building.

The New Testament Principle

We also need to see one more confirmation, that is, that today the church is the body of Christ (Eph. 1:23; 1 Cor. 12:12). It is not a physical body. Today the church is also the house of God. This house is not a physical house; God dwells in this house today. First Timothy 3:15 tells us that the church is the house of the living God. This house is composed of living persons and we consider the church as our home. The church is our home and this home is not built with cement, redwood, or Arizona stone. We have a home built spiritually with the living believers. Thus, today the church is a home—not a physical home but a home composed with living persons. The New Testament principle is the eternal principle. The Old Testament principle is the principle in typology and is temporary. However, the New Testament principle, being eternal, will exist forever going through the millennium and on into eternity. This principle is that God's dwelling in His economy is not a physical building, but a building built up with living persons. Such a principle along with our logical consideration would not allow us to interpret the New Jerusalem as a physical city. If you interpret the New Jerusalem in this way, you are going against the basic principles of the New Testament and you are against the principles which are eternal.

THE NEW JERUSALEM IN HEBREWS

Based upon this kind of understanding, let us read some more verses in the book of Hebrews concerning the New Jerusalem. In Hebrews 12:18-21 we see some things in the background: "For you have not come to the mountain which might be touched and which was set on fire, and to darkness and gloom and whirlwind, and to the sound of a trumpet and to the voice of words, which those who heard entreated that no further word should be spoken to them; for they could not bear that which was commanded: If even a beast touch the mountain it shall be stoned. And so fearful was the sight, Moses said, I am terrified and trembling." We, the New Testament believers, have not come to these physical things—a physical Mount Sinai, the sound of a trumpet and a physical voice. Then verse 22 tells us that we have come to Mount Zion. Mount Zion is in the heavens. This verse does not say we shall come to Mount Zion, but it says we have come. We have come (perfect tense) to Mount Zion and to the city of the living God. The mount's name is Zion and the city's name is heavenly Jerusalem. We have also come to myriads of angels, to the universal gathering. The myriads of angels are the universal gathering. We have come to the church of the firstborn ones who have been enrolled in the heavens (v. 23). They are not in the heavens yet, but their names have been enrolled there. Hebrews 12:23 also tells us that we have come "to God the Judge of all, and to the spirits of just men who have been made perfect." The spirits of just men, who are the Old Testament saints, are in Paradise where Abraham is (Luke 16:22, 23, 25, 26) and where the Lord Jesus and the saved thief went after they died on the cross (Luke 23:43). Verse 24 continues to say that we have also come "to Jesus, the Mediator of the new covenant, and to the blood of sprinkling, which speaks better than that of Abel." There are eight items mentioned in Hebrews 12:22-24. The things mentioned in verses 22-24 are heavenly or spiritual, in contrast with the earthly and physical things listed in verses 18-19. Among these eight items is the New Jerusalem. All the items referred to in verses 22-24 should not be taken in a physical sense. We have never come to the physical blood of Jesus nor have we been sprinkled physically. No one among us has ever come to the physical blood of Jesus. This is another illustration to show us that we cannot understand the New Jerusalem in such a physical sense. Just as the blood in these verses cannot be understood in a physical sense, neither can the New Jerusalem in these verses be understood in this way. None of us has ever come to the blood of Jesus in a physical sense. It is also hard for us to locate the eight items in verses 22-24. The spirits of just men are in Paradise. Mount Zion is in the heavens; it cannot be interpreted in a physical sense. This discussion of these verses may help us to understand the Bible concerning the New Jerusalem.

Hebrews 11:14-16 says that Abraham and other Old Testament saints were expecting, were waiting, for a better country with a marvelous city. After considering these verses we must ask where Abraham is today. When the Lord Jesus was on this earth Abraham had not entered into this better country with the marvelous city because in Luke 16 the Lord told us definitely that Abraham at that time was in Hades. Where, though, is Abraham after the Lord's resurrection? Some Christian teachers taught us that when the Lord resurrected from Hades, He brought the entire paradise (a section of Hades) to the third heavens. According to this kind of teaching, Abraham should have entered into heaven, entered into the better country and to the city that he expected. At this point, we must read Hebrews 11:39: "And these all, having obtained testimony through their faith, did not obtain the promise." Paul wrote the book of Hebrews many years after the resurrection and the ascension of Christ. By this time Abraham had still not obtained the promise. According to the traditional teaching, Abraham entered into the heavenly country and into the good city, but Hebrews 11:39 tells us that at least thirty years after the ascension Abraham had still not obtained the promise. Some might say that this means Abraham entered into the country in the heavens but that the good city has not been completed. If this is the case then where would Abraham stay? Could it be that the Lord intended to finish millions of rooms in the heavenly mansion, but probably He only finished enough rooms to contain the Old Testament saints? On the one hand, according to the traditional teachings, the Lord in resurrection ascended to the heavens to build the mansion, and on the other hand, He moved Paradise to the third heavens. We must ask then where He has located all the Old Testament saints. I am illustrating this to show you how illogical and unscriptural the traditional teachings are. This is leaven! Many people take in the leaven without any consideration. I followed Brother Nee because he was the only person I saw who would not follow the traditional interpretations of the Bible which are illogical and unscriptural.

By the time Paul had written Hebrews 11, Abraham had still not obtained the promise, "God having in view something better concerning us, that apart from us they should not be made perfect" (v. 40). God had something better in view concerning the New Testament believers, that apart from us the Old Testament saints, including Abraham, should not be made perfect. Abraham is waiting to be perfected and he can never be perfected apart from us. This means that Abraham can never enter into that better country, into that marvelous city, apart from us.

When we will enter, he will enter and all the Old Testament saints will enter. Note 40[3] in Hebrews 11 says:

> Both the participation in the kingdom for one thousand years (Rev. 20:4, 6) and the sharing in the New Jerusalem for eternity (Rev. 21:2-3; 22:1-5) are a corporate matter. The kingdom feast will be for both the Old Testament and the New Testament overcomers (Matt. 8:11). The blessed New Jerusalem will be composed of both the Old Testament saints and the New Testament believers (Rev. 21:12-14). Hence, apart from the New Testament believers, the Old Testament ones cannot obtain what God has promised. For the obtaining and enjoying of the good things of God's promise, they need the perfection of the New Testament believers. Now they are waiting for us to go on that they may be perfected.

The Old Testament saints are waiting for us to be perfected so that they may enjoy the New Jerusalem with us.

THE TRIUNE GOD WROUGHT INTO HIS CHOSEN PEOPLE IN A FIVE-FOLD WAY

What we will enjoy together are not physical things, but we will enjoy the Triune God wrought into His chosen people in at least five ways. First, the Triune God is wrought into His chosen people as their Creator, their Redeemer, and their Regenerator to give them a threefold triune existence—created, redeemed, and regenerated. Second, the Triune God has been wrought into His redeemed for their being constituted with the divine nature for the building up of the New Jerusalem with gold, pearls, and precious stones. Third, the Triune God is His redeemed people's entry into the divine composition as the three gates on the four sides of the city. Fourth, He is for their living in the divine nature, in the divine tree, and in the divine river.

Lastly, He is for their enjoyment of the divine life as the light, the tree, and the river. The Triune God has been wrought into His redeemed people in these five ways: for their existence, for their constitution, for their entry into the divine composition, for their living in this composition, and for their enjoyment in this composition. The New Jerusalem is not a physical building. It is a composition of God's redeemed ones who have the Triune God wrought into them in these five ways. This is the very significance of the ultimate consummation of the entire Bible, of the entire revelation, of the entire Triune God, and of His entire economy. Abraham was waiting for such a blessing even though by that time he probably did not understand the fullness of such a blessing.

THE ULTIMATE CONSUMMATION OF LIFE

In the same way, today we have received eternal life but we do not understand what is involved in the blessing of the eternal life. In the New Jerusalem there is one main item of the ultimate consummation—the ultimate consummation of life. Based upon this, I would ask you young brothers to go back to study the Bible concerning the divine life. The Gospels tell us clearly that when we believe in the Lord Jesus, we receive eternal life. The Gospels also tell us that we need to inherit the eternal life (Matt. 19:29 cf. Luke 18:29-30). We must also know what the difference is between receiving the eternal life and inheriting the eternal life.

The Eternal Life in Three Stages

The eternal life as a blessing from God to us is in three stages. In the first stage we receive the eternal life and we enjoy the eternal life in this age. The second stage is in the manifestation of the kingdom of the heavens in the millennium, in the kingdom age, where we will inherit the eternal life. In the third stage it is not to receive nor to inherit the eternal life but to enjoy the eternal life in its consummation. In this age of grace the eternal life is for us to receive and then to live by. Then in the coming age of the kingdom the eternal life is for us to inherit. This life becomes our inheritence in the kingdom. We have seen that the divine life is the kingdom. When you inherit this eternal life, you inherit the kingdom. Finally, this eternal life will consummate in eternity in the new heaven and the new earth. There is the need of much study to find out what the blessings are in the receiving stage of the eternal life, in the inheriting stage of the eternal life, and in the consummating stage of the eternal life. I do not believe that such a study could be finished within half a year.

Probably Abraham did not know or realize the blessings he would inherit during his time. We must admit, though, that most of us do not know either what the eternal life will be to us in the millennium or what it will be to us in eternity. We just infer what it will be like by our natural mentality. The fact that we do not understand fully what is written in the Bible is shown by our ascribing the blessings to the peoples on the new earth in Revelation 21:3-4 to ourselves. To have the Lord wipe away our tears and the taking away of sorrows, crying, and pain is all according to our natural understanding. In Revelation 21:7, though, it indicates that God's sons will participate in the New Jerusalem with all its enjoyment. The Recovery Version of Revelation has clearly pointed out the differences between the blessings assigned to the unsaved nations and the blessings inherited by or consummating in the sons of God. This shows that in our understanding of the Bible and in our reading of the Bible we remain in our natural mentality. We do not desire to be transferred out of the natural kingdom into the spiritual kingdom. We mostly understand the verses in the Bible in the natural kingdom. We do not understand the divine word in the divine kingdom. This is the problem. Many teachers of the Bible have written many books according to the Bible concerning ethics, morality, human behavior, and the improvement of character. How many books, however, have we seen written concerning the blessings of the eternal life in the new heaven and the new earth as portrayed by the New Jerusalem? The New Jerusalem is a full portrait of the blessings of the eternal life to the fullest. It is the consummation of the eternal life in its fullest blessing. The eternal life is full of divine blessings. We have received the eternal life at the time of our regeneration and we are now living by it. We will inherit it as a kind of kingdom blessing, a blessing in full, in the millennium. Also, this life will consummate in its fullest blessing and this consummation ultimately is the New Jerusalem. We must see that the New Jerusalem is not a physical city, but that it is the ultimate consummation of the eternal life in its fullest blessing.

The Need of Our Study

Every aspect of the ultimately consummated eternal life needs our study. We must study based upon the last one and a half chapters in the Bible—Revelation 21 and the first half of Revelation 22. We must study this portion with the entire Bible as our reference, as our library. Do not go to other libraries. Also, the books that we have written and published over the years will help you study this portion of the word. I must say again that this New Jerusalem is not a physical building. It is the ultimate consummation of the eternal life which we have received and are still living by in its fullest blessing. The New Testament age is the age for us to receive this eternal life and to live by it. The second age, the age of the millennium, is the age for us to inherit the blessings of this eternal life in full as a kingdom. Then eternity will be the age for us to enjoy the ultimate consummation of all the blessings of this eternal life to the fullest. Therefore, the New Jerusalem is the ultimate consummation of this eternal life in its fullest blessing. If we understand this, this solves all our problems and answers all our questions concerning the New Jerusalem as a city of God to be our eternal portion.

A MUTUAL DWELLING—AN ETERNAL PRINCIPLE

We must remember that our God in His Trinity, with all His plan, economy, and achievements, has been wrought into this city. That means our God in His Trinity with everything He has done and achieved has been wrought into our intrinsic being. Therefore, He and we are blended, mingled together, as a mutual dwelling to Him and to us. He will dwell in us as His habitation, the eternal tabernacle, for eternity, and we will dwell in Him as our dwelling, the eternal temple, for eternity. There should be no consideration in our being that the New Jerusalem is a physical dwelling. Even today in the church age we care for the church as our home. To God the church is His house and to us it is our home. We should not interpret the church in a physical sense, but in the sense of persons. This home, the church, is in the same principle as the New Jerusalem. This home is the Triune God with all His achievements wrought into the believers' humanity. This home, the church, is a mingling of divinity with humanity. This principle is eternal. It will exist and be applied to the New Jerusalem. The church today is a house of the Triune God wrought into His redeemed ones as their home. The New Jerusalem will continue this principle. The only difference is that today we are in the process and in that day of the New Jerusalem it will be the consummation. The process to reach the consummation and the consummation itself are exactly the same in principle and in nature. Actually, the process is a precursor of the consummation and the consummation is a fulfillment of the precursor. These two are one item. Actually, we should praise the Lord that today we are already in the New Jerusalem. The church life is a miniature of the New Jerusalem.

THE MOTHER OF THE BELIEVERS

Galatians 4:24-26 is another portion from the Word which we must consider concerning the New Jerusalem:

"Which things are an allegory; for these are two cov-
enants, one from Mount Sinai, bringing forth children unto
slavery, which is Hagar. Now this Hagar is Mount Sinai in
Arabia, and corresponds to the Jerusalem which now is,
for she is in slavery with her children. But the Jerusalem
above is free, who is our mother." The physical Jerusalem
represents the law which produces children unto slavery,
but the Jerusalem which is above is free who is our mother.
In Revelation 21 the New Jerusalem is a wife, but here it is
the mother. Therefore, the New Jerusalem is a wife to be
our mother. If the New Jerusalem is a physical thing, how
could this city produce us as her children? How could our
begetting mother be a physical city built with real precious
stones, gold, and pearls? None of these items are organic.
Neither gold, nor pearls, nor precious stones produce
anything. Then how could they have children? These
verses again show us that we should not understand the
New Jerusalem in a physical sense. Only the natural,
uneducated mentality which possesses inadequate biblical
knowledge understands in this way. If our mind has ever
been renewed, has ever been enlightened, and if we have
been fully and adequately spiritually educated, we would
never understand the New Jerusalem in such a wrong and
superficial way.

The New Jerusalem, which is the Jerusalem above, the
heavenly Jerusalem, is our mother. This motherly Jerusalem
stands for grace. The physical Jerusalem stands for law,
and this heavenly Jerusalem which is our mother stands
for grace. In this grace are the Triune God, His plan, His
economy, His redemption, His salvation, and all His
achievements wrought into His chosen people. This is
grace in its totality and we all have been born of this
grace, so this grace is our mother. This surely could never
be a physical city. This must be the Triune God with His
redemption and His salvation, including regeneration,
transformation, and glorification, wrought into His chosen
ones. This is our mother and this is grace. We do not

belong to anything physical. We belong to this divine yet
human composition saturated, even constituted, with
God's grace which produces us all. The New Jerusalem is
our mother and we are her children.

I hope this principle will help us in understanding this
ultimate consummation. I also hope, trust, and expect
much of you younger brothers for the future. You must
study all the things I have given you. All these hints and
principles need our entire life to study. These principles are
very basic and very fundamental. This is the vision in the
Lord's recovery, which is not the teaching of theology, but
is fully based upon the New Testament ministry.

THE VISION CONCERNING THE NEW JERUSALEM— THE ULTIMATE CONSUMMATION

(5)

JOHN 14

I still feel that we need to see more concerning the New Jerusalem and this problem of interpreting it as a heavenly mansion by looking at John 14, an auxiliary chapter to Revelation 21 and 22. We must purge out this leaven of the heavenly mansion. To understand John 14 through 16 plus chapter seventeen as a prayer, we need to know how the entire Gospel of John is arranged. To know any point, especially a serious point in the Bible, we must take care of the entire book in which it is located. Then we know where that point is and how it is related to the context of the entire book.

JOHN 1-11

The Gospel of John has an initial, complete section of eleven chapters. Chapter one gives us an introduction, a prologue, of the entire book. This prologue provides a clear view of the book of John. Then in chapter two are the principle of life and the goal of life. Then nine cases are presented to us from chapter three through chapter eleven—from the case of regeneration with Nicodemus through the case of resurrection with Lazarus. All of these cases are quite meaningful. They give us a clear view of how this life which Christ imparts into people meets the need of every man's case.

JOHN 12

Chapter twelve begins a new section. In this section the first part is a feast, a fellowship, in a small home in Bethany. That house in Bethany gives us a picture of the miniature of the church life. In chapter twelve the church life is portrayed in a miniature way because after all the instances of the divine life meeting the need of every man's case, the church life is produced.

In chapter twelve we also see the feast of the Passover (v. 12). Many people, even from abroad, came to Jerusalem to keep this feast. When they came they heard about the greatest miracle, the resurrection of Lazarus from among the dead (12:17-18). Many people were excited and wanted to see the one who had performed this miracle (v. 19). Therefore, the name of Jesus became widely spread and famous. At that juncture, Jesus entered into Jerusalem in a lowly and humble way, yet the people gave Him the top welcome. Humanly speaking, according to the natural concept, this was a golden time for Jesus when He was on the earth. All the people welcomed Him and a number of people wanted to see Him. They thought that Jesus would be happy, but His answer indicated just the opposite (12:23-28). It indicated that He did not care for that big welcome. That was not the thing on His heart and that was not the thing in which He was interested.

THE WAY OF JESUS' GLORIFICATION

From John 12:20 to the end of chapter seventeen is a separate section which could be titled: "The Way of Jesus' Glorification." The glorification of Jesus is also mentioned in chapter seven. Chapter seven tells us that whoever believes in the Lord shall drink of Him and shall have rivers of living water flowing out of his innermost being. These rivers refer to the Spirit and this Spirit was not yet because Jesus was not yet glorified (vv. 37-39). In the Gospel of John, the glorification of Jesus is a major point to which many readers and Bible teachers have not paid adequate attention. Chapter twelve tells us that the people gave Him a big welcome and that to them it was exciting to see Jesus (v. 13). It was at this juncture that the Lord spoke something which indicated that he was not interested in that kind of welcome, in that kind of exaltation, but that He was burdened to go through a procedure that He might be glorified.

We need to read some of the verses in chapter twelve and in chapters fourteen through seventeen in order to have a clear view of this matter of glorification. "Now there were certain Greeks among those who were going up that they might worship at the feast. These then came to Philip, who was from Bethsaida of Galilee, and asked him, saying, Sir, we wish to see Jesus. Philip came and told Andrew; Andrew came, and Philip, and they told Jesus" (12:20-22). Jesus did not answer Andrew and Philip by saying, "Hallelujah! Glorious!" Instead we read in verse 23, "And Jesus answered them, saying, The hour has come for the Son of Man to be glorified." This is the subject of the following chapters through chapter seventeen. If we are going to understand chapters fourteen through seventeen we must stand on this key verse. This verse is the ground and base for interpreting John 14 through 17. After chapter seventeen, He was betrayed, arrested, judged and sentenced to death, crucified, buried, and resurrected. Then He came back in glorification. From 12:20 to the end of chapter seventeen is an unveiling of how Jesus could be glorified. Then from chapter eighteen through chapter twenty Jesus was glorified through death and resurrection. In resurrection and on the day of resurrection, He came back to His disciples not in the natural way but in the resurrected way. In other words, in the glorified way He came as the glorified Jesus.

Then in the verse following 12:23 the Lord Jesus unveils the way for Him to be glorified: "Truly, truly, I say to you, unless a grain of wheat falls into the ground and dies, it abides alone; but if it dies, it bears much fruit." This is the way for Jesus to be glorified—to die and to be resurrected to bring forth many grains. These many grains actually are the essence of His glorification. Within a small grain of wheat is the life element. When the life within it is released to bear much fruit, the many grains become the glorification of the one grain. The more grains which are produced, the more glory the one grain enjoys. To die and to grow up in resurrection was the way for Jesus, as the one grain with the divine life concealed in His humanity, to be glorified. His humanity was a shell to Him just like the grain of wheat has a shell which must be broken through death. The human shell of our Lord's humanity had to be broken so that the divine life concealed within Him could be released to grow up to produce many grains for Him to be glorified.

After the Lord responded to Andrew and Philip, He prayed in verse 28, "Father, glorify your name." The Father's name denotes His Person. The Lord was asking the Father to glorify His Person, because the very divine Person of the Father had been concealed in His humanity. After Jesus prayed, "Father, glorify your name," there came a voice out of heaven, "I have both glorified it, and will glorify it again." This is the Lord's prayer on the way to His being glorified. Then in verses 32 and 33 He said, "And I, if I be lifted up from the earth, will draw all men to Myself. Now He said this signifying the kind of death He was about to die." The Lord's death and His resurrection would produce much fruit, and this fruit would be the many men drawn to Christ by His wonderful death. When He died, all men would be drawn to Him and these men drawn to Him would be the very fruit produced by Him in resurrection.

John 13:31-32 says, "Then when he [Judas] went out, Jesus said, Now is the Son of Man glorified, and God is glorified in Him. If God is glorified in Him, God will also glorify Him in Himself, and will glorify Him immediately."

At the feast of the Passover the Lord Jesus exposed Judas and indicated to Peter and John that Judas was the one who was going to betray Him (13:23-27). At the end of the feast of the Passover and before the setting up of the Lord's table, Judas was exposed. As a Jew, Judas had a right to participate in the feast of the Passover, but he was not a genuine regenerated believer so he did not have the right to participate in the Lord's table. He was exposed and at that juncture he left. Then he went out to see the Pharisees to carry out his betrayal. While the Lord Jesus was setting up His table, Judas was carrying out his betrayal to bring those Jewish opposers to the garden of Gethsemane.

When Judas left, Jesus said, "Now is the Son of Man glorified, and God is glorified in Him" (13:31). This meant that the very inner essence of the man Jesus would be released through His death, and when He is released and the Father is released within Him, God is glorified—"If God is glorified in Him, God will also glorify Him in Himself, and will glorify Him immediately" (13:32). These words concerning glorification refer to His death and resurrection. His death and His resurrection was a glorification to Him. The glorification of Jesus is His multiplication—the one grain being multiplied into many grains. This is also His expansion, His enlargement. He was expanded, enlarged, multiplied, in His death and resurrection, and that multiplication was His glorification.

After this the Lord went to the garden of Gethsemane according to the record of the synoptic Gospels, Matthew, Mark, and Luke. According to John, however, after this the Lord did not go directly to the garden of Gethsemane. He gave a long discourse recorded in John covering three chapters plus a long prayer in chapter seventeen. Most Bible readers realize that John 14 through 16 comprises the Lord Jesus' last talk with His disciples while He was on this earth on the night of His betrayal. After this talk and the prayer, He and the disciples went to the garden of

Gethsemane where He was arrested. This fellowship should make us clear concerning the context of chapters fourteen through seventeen.

JOHN 17

After the Lord spoke that long discourse in chapters fourteen through sixteen, He prayed a prayer in chapter seventeen. The first verse in this chapter is quite crucial: "These things Jesus spoke, and lifting up His eyes to heaven, He said, Father, the hour has come; glorify Your Son that the Son may glorify You." This word matches John 12:23 where the Lord said, "The hour has come for the Son of Man to be glorified." The only difference is that here that word has become a prayer. The Lord prayed that the Father might glorify Him that He might glorify the Father. For many years I could not understand what the main subject of the Lord's prayer in chapter seventeen was. Now we can see that the subject of this long prayer is the glorification of Jesus.

The Issue of Jesus Being Glorified

In 17:21 the Lord prayed, "That they all may be one; even as You, Father, are in Me and I in You, that they also may be in Us, that the world may believe that You have sent Me." The issue of Jesus being glorified is that His believers will be brought into the Triune God, into the divine "Us." There is a coinherence in the divine Trinity. In this verse the Lord says that the Father is in Him and that He is in the Father. This is the coinherence of the divine Trinity, and this coinherence has to be applied to His believers that all His believers may be in the divine Us, in the divine Trinity. This is the issue of the glorification of Jesus.

Where Jesus Is

John 17:24 says, "Father, I desire that those whom You have given Me may also be with Me where I am." Now we have to ask where Jesus is. John 14:3 says, "And if I go and prepare a place for you, I am coming again and will receive you to Myself, that where I am you also may be." Many Christian readers and teachers unconsciously change the word Myself in this verse to heaven—"I will receive you to heaven." However, the Lord says that He will receive the believers not to heaven but to Himself that where He is they also may be. Also, many Christian teachers say that He is in the heavens that we also may be in the heavens. This is their interpretation. To answer the question of where the Lord is, we must let the Lord Jesus Himself answer. In verse 10 of the same chapter, chapter fourteen, the Lord says, "Do you not believe that I am in the Father, and the Father is in Me?" Where is the Lord? He is in the Father. He was going to prepare a place for the disciples that where He was they also might be. He is in the Father so that we may also be there in the Father. He was going to prepare a place through His death and resurrection to bring us into the Father. His death and resurrection was His preparation to bring us into the Father in whom He was. Then where He is, we may be also. He said this at the beginning of chapter fourteen in verse 3 and He prayed about this at the end of chapter seventeen in verse 24. In verse 24 the Lord says, "Father, I desire that those whom You have given Me may also be with Me where I am." The Lord was saying, "I am in You, Father, but they are not. I desire that they all may be in You as I am, that they may be with Me in You." "That they may behold My glory which You have given Me, for You have loved Me before the foundation of the world" (17:24). The glory in this verse is the glory to be the Son of God, possessing God's life to express God. This is the glory of Jesus. He has given us this glory and now we are all the sons of God possessing God's life to express God Himself.

In John 14:20 the Lord tells us that in the day of resurrection "you shall know that I am in My Father, and you in Me, and I in you." The Lord is in the Father and we are in Him, so we are in the Father by being in Him. This could transpire by His death and resurrection.

THE MANY ABODES—THE LOVERS OF JESUS

Then 14:23 says, "Jesus answered and said to him, If anyone loves Me, he will keep My word, and My Father will love him, and We will come to him and make an abode with him." The Son and the Father through the Spirit come to the lover of Jesus to make an abode with him. In 14:2 the Lord said, "In My Father's house are many abodes." What are the abodes? The abodes according to verse 23 are the believers, the lovers of Jesus.

MY FATHER'S HOUSE

Now we must go on to ask what the Lord meant when He said "My Father's house" in 14:2. This truth has been thoroughly leavened. After being leavened, this point has befuddled nearly all the Christians. They interpret the Father's house as the heavenly mansion. In order to see what the Father's house is in this verse we must go back to chapter two where the Father's house was already mentioned. John 2:16 says, "And to those who were selling the doves He said, Take these things away; do not make My Father's house a house of merchandise." The same term, My Father's house, has been used in the book of John twice. Its first mention in chapter two indicates God's temple, not the heavenly mansion. The Lord goes on to say in verse 19, "Destroy this temple, and in three days I will raise it up." Then verse 21 says, "But He spoke of the temple of His body." Now we can see from John 2 that "My Father's house" is God's temple and God's temple is the Body of Christ. "When therefore He was raised from among the dead, His disciples remembered that He said this, and they believed the Scripture and the word which Jesus has spoken" (v. 22). We need to read verse 19 again: "Jesus answered and said to them, Destroy this temple, and in three days I will raise it up." In resurrection Jesus rose up with all His believers. First Peter 1:3 tells us that all the Lord's believers were resurrected in Jesus' resurrection. Therefore, the man Jesus was killed and destroyed as a smaller temple, but Jesus with all His believers were resurrected to be the larger and mystical Body of Christ. This mystical Body is the temple, and this temple is "My Father's house." This is the right way to interpret the Bible. "My Father's house" in 14:2 must be interpreted based upon chapter two of the same book where "My Father's house" is God's temple and where God's temple is the Body of Christ.

The Multiplication of Jesus—His Glorification

John 12 shows us the expansion, the increase, the multiplication of Jesus. One man was killed, but in resurrection He was no longer merely one man. One grain was sown into the earth, but after growing up it remains no longer one grain. It becomes many grains which are the multiplication of the one grain; this is the real expansion of Jesus to be His mystical Body. His glorification is His multiplication and His multiplication is His expansion from one Person to a corporate Body. Also, this one Person with His corporate Body is the house of His Father. In the Epistles we are told clearly that the church is the house of the living God (1 Tim. 3:15). After looking at all these verses, we can see that the house in John 14 actually refers to the church.

Then in 14:3 we can see what the Lord Jesus means by saying that He was going and that while He was going, He was coming. In 14:3 the Lord says "If I go ... I am coming." This means that the Lord's going (through His death and resurrection) is His coming (to His disciples—vv. 18, 28). Through His death and resurrection Jesus has been multiplied. He has been expanded. He brought forth many believers which are the many grains who are the members of His Body, which is God's house. According to the context of the sections of the Gospel of John, the Father's house must be interpreted in this way. To interpret it in another way would be according to the natural, religious concept and according to the traditional teaching.

It is crucial that we see the matter of glorification in these chapters. John 12:24 unveils His multiplication in which we see one grain becoming many grains. This was the time for the Son of Man to be glorified, so His multiplication is His glorification. His multiplication is to produce many grains for making a loaf and that loaf signifies the mystical Body of Christ, which is today the house of the living God. This house will consummate in the New Jerusalem. Both the New Jerusalem and the church are God's dwelling place.

The Eternal Principle

The eternal principle is applied to the church and also applied to the New Jerusalem. The eternal principle is this: the Triune God has wrought Himself into His chosen and redeemed people to be their existence, to be their entrance into the eternal kingdom of God, to be their constitution, to be their living, and to be their enjoyment. These items are not only in the ultimate consummation, in the New Jerusalem, but also in the book of John and in the Epistles for our present enjoyment and experience.

Do you not have the Triune God, the Creator, the Redeemer, and the Regenerator, as the source of your existence? Surely you do. Do you not have the Triune God as your entrance into the spiritual and divine realm? Surely you do. Are you not now under the constitution of the Triune God? The Father's nature as the gold, the Son in His redemptive work as the pearl, and the Spirit's transforming work as the precious stone are all our present experience. Paul tells us in 1 Corinthians 3 that we need to build the church with gold, silver, and precious stones. This is something we are presently enjoying. Are we not living by the Triune God as our street, our way, as our food, and as our drink? Surely we are. Are we not enjoying the Triune God as our light, as our tree of life, and as our river of life? We are surely in the up-to-date experience of this enjoyment. All this is here today in the church and all this will consummate in the coming New Jerusalem for eternity. This principle is eternal. Therefore, the Father's house is God's dwelling in the New Testament age which is the church of Christ. This will consummate eventually in the new heaven and the new earth in the New Jerusalem. In the church today, and in the New Jerusalem in the eternal age, the principle is the same. In its intrinsic essence the church in this age is the same as the New Jerusalem in eternity.

THE FATHER'S HOUSE, THE VINE TREE, THE NEWBORN CHILD, AND THE ONENESS

In John 14 the Father's house is a corporate matter, comprising all the believers who are in Christ. Then in chapter fifteen is a vine tree, which is again a corporate matter showing us how we are in Christ, the vine tree, and how Christ is in us, the branches. In chapter sixteen we see a newborn child (v. 21). This newborn child is Jesus born as the firstborn Son of God in His resurrection (Acts 13:33; Hebrews 1:5; Romans 1:4). This newborn child includes Jesus as the Head and all His members who have been resurrected with Him. They become the members of this newborn child. Actually, this newborn child refers to the birth of the new man in Ephesians 2:15. In the concluding prayer in John 17 is the oneness. The very oneness in chapter seventeen equals the newborn child, which equals the vine tree, which equals the house. These are the same items in different aspects.

The house in chapter fourteen, the vine tree in chapter fifteen, the newborn child in chapter sixteen, and the oneness in chapter seventeen are realized by the Triune God wrought into the very being of all the believers as the very source and substance of their existence, as their entrance into this divine realm, as the very essences for their constitution, their building up, as their living, and as their enjoyment. By this the house is built, the tree is growing, the new child is born, and the oneness is practical. This is basically and intrinsically the very essence of the New Testament ministry.

TRADITIONAL THEOLOGY VERSUS THE NEW TESTAMENT MINISTRY

The traditional Christian understanding is that Jesus as the Son of God was sent by the Father and died on the cross for our sins. He was resurrected and ascended to the heavens and the Spirit was sent down to inspire us to believe in Him. The believers believed and they were forgiven, justified, redeemed, and saved. These believers were also regenerated. Then when the believers die they go to the place which the Lord Jesus promised that He was going to prepare in John 14. This place is an absolutely objective, physical thing to them which has nothing to do with their present life. Eventually, according to this interpretation, that mansion will be the New Jerusalem, the holy city. This will be the eternal dwelling place of all the believers. We can see that this kind of understanding is altogether objective and nothing of it is related to life. In much of today's traditional theology they do not even talk about life that much.

We need to check with ourselves in this matter. Are we preachers, teachers, and ministers of the Word in the Lord's recovery in this way? Doctrinally you may say no, but practically you have never stayed away from that kind of objective theology. This kind of theology is altogether off from the New Testament ministry. The New Testament ministry does not minister such an objective theology. It ministers the Triune God passing through the necessary processes (incarnation, human living, crucifixion, resurrection and ascension) and becoming the all-inclusive life-giving Spirit to impart Himself into our very being to give us a new existence, to become our entrance into a new realm, and to become our very intrinsic essence for our new constitution in the Body of Christ. Also, this very processed Triune God is now our life, our living, our way, and our enjoyment, and we have to grow in this life unto maturity, unto the ultimate consummation of the eternal life, which is the New Jerusalem. This is the New Testament ministry.

Traditional theology and the New Testament ministry are absolutely in two different realms, in two kingdoms with two lives. One is the kingdom of objective theology, which is in a line having nothing to do with life. The second one, which is the spiritual one, the one that is ministered by the New Testament ministry, is a kingdom of the Triune God as life and everything to His chosen people; this is altogether in the line of life.

We must realize that if we minister something of the first realm, the realm of objective theology, apparently what we minister is scriptural and there is nothing against the Bible, but this kind of ministry sows the seed of wrong understanding which delays the saints growth in life and which holds them back and distracts them. This kind of objective theology also misleads people. Actually, this is very, very serious. It may not be that you intentionally do something to sow the seed of wrong understanding. You may have no intention of doing that. Your intention is firstly to save people and then to edify them—"to help people to grow." Actually, however, this kind of ministry is not the ministry of the New Testament.

A CRUCIAL MATTER

I do believe that the Lord has given us a new view of John 14 through 17. This is not a matter of doctrinal debate, but a crucial matter concerning the divine life. The house in John 14 and the New Jerusalem in Revelation 21 and 22 are very crucial points. If we interpret the house in John 14 as the heavenly mansion and the New Jerusalem in Revelation 21 and 22 as a physical city for the believers to lodge in with God, we kill the New Testament ministry. This interpretation takes away the heart and kills the pulse of the New Testament ministry. Through this wrong interpretation the New Testament ministry becomes "an empty corpse." This is not a debatable matter over doctrine. This is a crucial matter concerning the eternal life in which we must live today. We must realize that our destiny is the same way we live today with the Triune God in a five-fold way: the Triune God wrought into our being as our substance, as our entrance, as our constitution, as our living, and as our enjoyment. This is not a small matter. I hope that all of you will be saturated with this and soaked in this. Then you will minister nothing but the New Testament ministry. Even I hope that you brothers will preach the gospel in a new way, in the "New Jerusalem way." Do not follow traditional theology. Put out some messages for the gospel from the New Jerusalem. You must believe that your listeners will be able to understand. They were created by God in this way. When you preach the items from the New Jerusalem, you will touch their God-created nature. They will understand and they will be saved in an intrinsic and basic life way. If you are a soldier in today's United States army you must learn many new scientific things. It is not sufficient just to know how to use a rifle. This is too old. This would mean that as a soldier you are out of date. Today we are in the Lord's up-to-date recovery. I do believe the Lord has been with us by His mercy. This is the Lord's up-to-date recovery and I do beg you to review these messages, especially the last two messsages, again and again.

THE NEED OF A VISION

My burden in these messages is to show you the vision of the Lord's recovery today. I am not giving you a way to learn or some doctrines to get converted to. What you need is a vision with a thorough realization that the traditional theology and that much of the knowledge of the traditional doctrine are altogether a covering. Your natural concept, the doctrines that you have learned of the past, even the doctrines you have learned in the Lord's recovery, are veils that cover you from seeing something further. You must remember the Lord's word in Matthew 5:3: "Blessed are the poor in spirit." This word was spoken to the self-satisfied Jewish leaders who were loaded with their Jewish doctrines, Jewish theology, knowledge of the law, and knowledge of the Old Testament things. They were loaded and full of these items. Therefore, the opening word on the mount was that they needed to be poor in their spirit. Perhaps we are full of traditional theology, our natural, religious mentality, and ethics. We could also be full of character improvement, doctrines that we have been holding for years to seek spirituality and victory, and many other items. All these are veils. Many Christian teachers have been veiled and held back from going on to see what the Lord has shown us in these years, especially to see what is in John 14 and what the New Jerusalem is. There is no seeing of these things because many are self-satisfied. If you desire to go further and deeper into these mysterious truths, you must spend much time and much energy and pray much. This means you need to pay a price. You cannot pick up the things covered in the Life-studies so easily. Without the paying of a price in this kind of way, you can never go further.

As we have seen, John 14 through 17 is a section of the word on the multiplication of Jesus, that is, the glorification. The vine tree with its expansion of all the branches is the multiplication and glorification of Jesus. The newborn child in chapter sixteen as a corporate new man, with Jesus Christ as the Head and all the regenerated saints as the Body, fits in with the thought, the concept, of multiplication and glorification. Even the oneness prayed for by the Lord Jesus that all the believers would be one by being in the Triune God in chapter seventeen is the multiplication and the glorification of Jesus. If we interpret

"My Father's house" in John 14:2 as a physical mansion in the heavens, where would it belong in this section? It would be altogether a foreign body. The thought and the concept of such a thing is foreign to this section. It does not fit the context at all. It has nothing to do with the multiplication and glorification of the Lord Jesus. The only way to interpret "My Father's house" so that it fits the context and the thought of the Lord's multiplication and glorification is to see that this house is the mystical Body of Christ as His multiplication, His increase, to be God's house today. This does not only fit the context but it also becomes a key to open up the entire chapter of John 14. If you are going to understand and get into the depth of chapter fourteen you need such a key—the key of interpreting My Father's house as the very mystical Body of Christ to be God's dwelling today which will consummate in His eternal dwelling, the New Jerusalem.

Merely for you to learn how to present this matter is not what we are stressing. You need to see such a thing and this seeing will reconstitute you. This is not a matter of learning doctrine. You must be constituted with this vision. Then automatically you will carry out God's New Testament economy just as the Lord did in the four Gospels, just as the early apostles did in Acts, and just as Paul, Peter, and John wrote in all their writings. Then you will be fully governed, controlled, and directed by such a vision, and you will be restricted in the straight, central lane with its focus of the New Testament ministry. This is what we need.

THE VISION CONCERNING THE NEW JERUSALEM— THE ULTIMATE CONSUMMATION

(6)

Editor's Note: Those who were attending the elders' training were asked by Brother Lee to come to the Saturday morning meeting of February 11, 1984 thirty minutes earlier for prayer. The following word on prayer was given at the conclusion of that thirty-minute period.

A WORD CONCERNING OUR PRAYER

I did my best to enter into your prayers, but I could not make it. I would like to say frankly that your prayers were not prayers in a corporate way. All of you prayed individualistically. This is something of the old tradition. We must learn to come to a prayer meeting to pray as a body, a corporate body. To pray in the spiritual realm must be something corporate. Even in the worldly realm, to play football with eleven members on your team or basketball with five members on your team is not done individualistically, but in a corporate way. I was waiting, watching, and seeking a time for over half an hour that I could enter into your prayer, but I could not see what your line or what your goal was. Everyone who prayed had his own mind, his own goal. This is altogether due to our traditional background. I hope we all can realize that this morning we had a prayer meeting without a line, without a goal. We just came together to express our own feeling.

A long prayer always kills the prayer meeting. A long prayer indicates that you only care for yourself and that you do not care for others. You only care for your feeling; you do not care for the atmosphere and the flow in the meeting. When we come together to pray, you should not be the flow but the Spirit should. You should not be the line but the Spirit should. You should not be the goal but the Spirit should. We all must hold such an attitude with such a spirit that we are not the center, the flow, the line, the goal, but the Lord, the Spirit, is. Therefore, we are open— open to the Lord and open to the Spirit. If He would use us to start a prayer, maybe we would pray for just two seconds. We would not pray a long prayer to express our opinion, our feeling. Perhaps we have the inner feeling that this meeting of prayer should begin with the Lord's mercy. Then maybe we would pray, "Lord have mercy upon us. Thank You, Lord. Thank You that Your mercy can reach much farther than Your grace." This is good enough. The Lord just uses us this much to open the prayer meeting with His mercy.

If we were not following the way from our traditional background and if we were following the living Spirit instantly, no one would pray a long prayer full of doctrinal points. The prayer meeting does not need that. The prayer meetings needs a lot of instant, fresh inspiration with fresh points. This fresh inspiration is news, even the heavenly news. We all would pray one after another just like a team in a ball game. The members of one team play with one ball. This morning, however, everyone who prayed had their own ball. When I came in, I did not know "which ball I should catch." How many teams were here this morning? It seemed as if everybody was a team.

Do not think that I am too strict. We are here in the Lord's training and we are the leading ones. We are the so-called co-workers and the entire recovery of the Lord is in our hands. Yet we the leading ones were holding a prayer meeting in such a way. Since this is the case, what could we expect of the church prayer meetings? From our prayer it seems that we have never been in the Lord's recovery. We are merely a group of Christians coming together to pray, but seemingly not something in the Lord's recovery. I must tell you truthfully that I was very much disappointed by the prayer meeting this morning.

When some of you brothers stand up to give a testimony you like to preach. When you pray you also preach. When you speak it is always something long—a long prayer, a long testimony, and long sharing. This indicates that you probably have never dropped the old traditions. I would like to hear many of you stand up and share just two sentences. Do not tell a story, do not explain the reason why you did something, and do not present your knowledge. When some of you brothers were with us, I was always afraid of your beginning to speak either in the testing in the training or in giving a testimony. When you give a testimony, you always like to give a message full of stories at the end and at the beginning. You even pray in the same way. This shows that you have kept the oldness throughout the years. You brothers need to learn to stand up and show people "the diamond" in your testimony. You do not need to tell people that you bought the diamond from Hong Kong and that its expense forced you to borrow the money from your cousin and from your father. You do not need to tell us a story. You do not need to teach us or preach to us concerning what the diamond is and how you acquired it. This is wasting time. This is the oldness. Just take out the diamond and show it to others: "See this diamond. Do you like it? You can get it. Praise the Lord." This kind of testimony is good enough. I am speaking to you in an allegorical way, but I believe you understand the point. In the same way, long prayers kill the prayer meeting. Your long prayer tests people's patience. Your prayer tests how long people's endurance will last. Brothers, we must drop the old way.

Do you believe that when the one hundred twenty met

together in Jerusalem in Acts 1 that they prayed in our way? If they had prayed in this way I am sure they would have been tired and bored after ten days. The element of our traditional background could still be seen here this morning. I am not too strict. I feel that since we are in the training, I must be honest to all of you.

We must learn to forget all the things we have, all the things we know, and even all the things we have heard recently. Let us come together to pray with an open spirit with nothing occupying us; just come to the prayer meeting in an empty way. We should come to the prayer meeting with our whole being on the altar so the Lord can operate within us and even expose us. We should come to the prayer meeting with the attitude that we do not know anything but that we only know the Lord Himself. I want to assure all of you that if you would continue to use your old doctrine, your old knowledge, and your old experience or anything old you are through in the Lord's recovery. The Lord's recovery has nothing to do with anything old. "Re" means anew; it means to renew or to be new. It is not to be strange, peculiar, or odd, but to be new.

After we had been here together for five days I was very burdened last night to call this prayer meeting for this morning. I expected that our oldness would be killed in the last five days. We should have come to this prayer meeting this morning very empty and very new. Our attitude should have been that we know nothing, that we have nothing, that we are nothing. Even if we are something, that does not mean anything. If you had presented yourself to the Lord in such an open, empty way the Lord would touch you instantly. I do not believe that He would touch you to pray for three minutes. He would just touch you with a feeling which could be expressed in two seconds. This is good enough. This is very living! If you would open up your mouth and speak two or three sentences from within in this way, the entire heaven would be open. Not one of you can deny that after thirty minutes of your praying together this morning no one among us had the feeling that the heavens were opened. There was no open heaven. The more you prayed, the more clouds were brought in. There was a cloudy sky due to your prayer. I do not care who is right or who is wrong. I only care for the fact that this morning in our prayer we did not have a clear sky above us. My fellowship with you this morning is a part of this training.

I have been together with some of you for over fifteen years. Your coming here has always been a test to me. I have been very much tested by your way of speaking, praying, testifying, and sharing. I do not mean that we only say, "Praise the Lord! Amen! Hallelujah!" I mean that we must practice to live in our spirit. In the Lord's recovery we practice one thing—to live in spirit. We should not live in the old way of prayer, nor should we follow the old way of prayer. We must live in spirit and walk according to spirit. Your long prayer is altogether according to your knowledge, to your hearing, and to your kind of realization. There is no Spirit there. There are a lot of sentences full of wasted words. I would say that nearly your entire prayer was a waste; It was just to express your kind of feeling. This is not a prayer meeting. I say again that a prayer meeting should be like a team. All the members of the team are on the alert to play with one ball. You should pray in a way that the next one who prays can continue your prayer. If you played ball in such a way that no one could continue playing, you would be off the team.

Many among us here have been in the Lord's recovery for over thirty years, but this morning some of us were silent and did not pray and others prayed in a long way. We should not think that the ones who prayed were wrong and that the ones who did not pray were not wrong. I must ask those of you who did not pray why you would not pray. Did the Spirit lead you not to pray? I must also ask those of you who prayed if the Spirit led you to pray. I think with both questions the answer is no. You prayed and the Spirit did not lead you to pray; you did not pray and the Spirit did not lead you not to pray. Therefore, we all came here and behaved in ourselves and in our old way.

The experienced ones among us have learned to be "wise." The wisest way is not to open up your mouth. If you open your mouth, you will get in trouble. This morning, however, I am giving trouble not only to the ones who opened their mouths, but even more to the ones who did not open their mouths. Neither of you were right. The praying ones were not right. The ones who did not pray were even more not right. Therefore, we all have killed the prayer meeting this morning. We must learn from this. If the ones who did not pray had prayed in a short way, they would have taken over the prayer meeting, leaving no gap for the long prayers to creep in. If eleven members on a team are playing football and nine of these members are strong, they would take over the entire play and the two weaker ones would be left there. The game would still be quite good. I hope this fellowship will help us for the future.

REVELATION—A BOOK OF CONSUMMATION
(PART 1)

Since we have touched the ultimate consummation, the New Jerusalem, in the book of consummation, Revelation, I feel that it is best to see this ultimate consummation in this book in a more thorough way. We are not merely studying the Bible, nor are we debating any doctrine. We want to see what is in the ultimate consummation of God's entire revelation. The ultimate word of any writing is the final word, the concluding word, and the final, concluding word always gives us the real significance of that writing. Thousands of items were covered in the first sixty-five books of the Bible. These books cover a long span of time and many, many items. This always confuses the readers of the Bible. If the Bible were only three pages long, we could never be confused. But here are sixty-five books covering a long span of time and thousands and thousands of items. After reading this, it is easy to get lost. Therefore, in God's wisdom, He put all these items together in a consummating book; this is the last book, the sixty-sixth book of the Bible.

The last book is not a new book, but a harvest. Most of the new things in the Bible were there in Genesis. Genesis is a book of new items. Before the book of Genesis there was no creation. When creation came into being, that was something really new. Before Genesis, there was no man and only God was there in eternity; nothing had come into existence. The angels were not there and man was not there. Everything in Genesis was new. Before Genesis there was no Abraham, no Isaac, and no Jacob. The things in Genesis were new and sown into the field of God's revelation. Everything that was sown in the book of Genesis began to grow from the second book, Exodus, throughout the next sixty-four books of the Bible. Then the sixty-sixth book, Revelation, the last book of the entire Bible, is there as a harvest of the truths which were sown in Genesis. One verse in the book of Revelation tells us that "the harvest of the earth is ripe" (14:15). The time has come for the Lord to reap the harvest. The seeds of this harvest were sown in Genesis. Even the word Genesis means beginning. Genesis is a record of the beginning. Revelation is a book of harvest. The sowing of the seeds and their growth and development are over. Now is the harvest in Revelation. Actually, harvest is an interpretation of the word consummation. Consummation and harvest are synonyms. Our burden is to see all the items which are consummated in the book of Revelation.

A number of things in the Old Testament, though, are not consummated in the book of Revelation. All the consummations in Revelation are a consummation concerning Christ, concerning the Spirit, concerning life, and concerning the church. Many things in the Old Testament are consummated in Revelation which are seemingly not related to Christ, the Spirit, life, and the church. Actually they are all indirectly related. As we have seen, chapters four through twenty of Revelation are on God's universal, governmental administration. Seemingly, God's governmental administration has nothing to do with the church, but it is indirectly related to the church. This is why I have previously given you seventeen instances of the mentioning of the church in these seventeen chapters.

The Divine Trinity

The opening word in the book of Revelation shows us the harvest of the prevailing divine Trinity. Revelation 1:4-5a says, "Grace to you and peace from Him who is, and who was, and who is coming, and from the seven Spirits who are before His throne, and from Jesus Christ, the faithful Witness, the Firstborn of the dead, and the Ruler of the kings of the earth." Undoubtedly, this is the divine Trinity, but we must see that the mentioning of the divine Trinity here is the consummation of the divine Trinity revealed firstly in Genesis 1:1, where the subject "God" is plural in number, and developed throughout the entire Bible. This definition of the divine Trinity in Revelation 1:4-5a implies the entire divine Trinity revealed in the Bible.

This title of the divine Trinity in Revelation is different from the title—the Father, the Son, and the Spirit—in Matthew 28:19. The Father, the Son, and the Spirit does not imply the entire Bible. However, Him who is, who was, and who is coming brings us back to the beginning of the divine revelation concerning the divine Trinity (Exo. 3:14-15). The Ruler of the kings of the earth implies the ending of the revelation concerning the divine Trinity. Also, in between these titles are the seven Spirits, the faithful Witness, and the Firstborn of the dead. The entire Bible is needed to interpret this consummation of the divine title of the divine Trinity. This is the consummation of the divine Trinity from the beginning of the divine revelation to its end, not in a particular way, but in an all-embracing way. At the beginning of the book of Revelation the divine Trinity is consummated in an all-embracing way, and at the end of Revelation we see the divine Trinity consummated in an all-inclusive way, but applied to us in a very substantial, practical, and living way. We have seen that the divine Trinity in Revelation 21 and 22 has consummated to the uttermost to be our existence, our entrance into the divine realm, our constitution, our living, and our enjoyment.

The Church

From seeing the divine Trinity in an all-embracing way in Revelation 1:4 we must go on to the seven churches. The seven churches are a consummation of the doctrine concerning the church. This is the consummation of the church, which was first mentioned by the Lord Jesus in Matthew 16:18 and where the seed of this truth was sown. Then this seed grew up in the Acts and was growing in the Epistles where it developed to the uttermost. Then the last book of the New Testament gives us the consummation of the church—the local churches. The book of Revelation, especially chapter one, does not continue the thought that the church is God's *ekklesia*, God's house, Christ's Body, Christ's fullness, the new man, the wife, the Bride of Christ, or the warrior. The church in Revelation 1 is consummated as the lampstands. The lampstands are the consummation of all the definitions of all the aspects of the church.

Probably many of us have never thought about the location of the lampstands. Where are the local churches—on earth or in heaven? Surely they are on earth because Revelation 1:11 tells us that the seven churches are seven cities. None of the local churches are in the heavens, but they are all physical, geographical locations. The local churches are on the earth. Now we must ask where the lampstands are. Are they in the heavens or on the earth?

We need to be careful in our answer to this question. The lampstands are the consummation of the lampstand in the Old Testament. In Exodus 25:31-38 and in Zechariah 4:2 the lampstand was in the tabernacle and in 1 Kings 7:49 the lampstand was in the temple. Is this location within the tabernacle the earthly place or the heavenly place? The earthly place was outside the tabernacle where the altar was. But what about within the tabernacle? The lampstand is not in the outer court but in the holy place. In practical existence the churches are on this earth. In the sign of the churches, the lampstands, the churches are in the holy place. Here the Son of Man, the Lord Jesus, appears not as a priest offering sacrifices on the altar outside of the tabernacle, but He appears as a priest who serves within the tabernacle to take care of the lampstands.

The priest in the Old Testament had a three-fold duty— to offer the sacrifices, to trim the lamps of the lampstands, and to burn the incense. One of their responsibilities was in the outer court and two were in the tabernacle. In the book of Revelation the Lord Jesus appears as a priest only with these two duties within the tabernacle—to trim the lampstand and to offer the incense (Rev. 8:3-5). There is not a verse in Revelation which indicates that the Lord is offering some sacrifice because the offering of sacrifices has already been accomplished. In chapter one He appears not as the priest offering the sacrifices, but as the priest trimming the lampstand. Therefore, we must realize that according to the lampstand, the churches are in the heavens. According to the practical existence, the churches are on the earth. This indicates that the churches are in the heavens appearing on the earth. This is the principle of Bethel, which is the house of God (Gen. 28:17, 19). The house of God is a spot where a ladder joins the earth to the heavens and brings the heavens down to the earth. As a consummation concerning the church, we see a view of how the church in its significance is in the heavens and in its physical existence is on the earth. Therefore, the church is a heavenly matter, yet it is on earth. This is the consummation. To understand Revelation 1 concerning the church as the lampstand, we need the entire Old Testament. The seven lampstands are the consummation of the lampstand in the Old Testament.

The Seven Stars

The seven stars in Revelation 1:16 and 20 are also a consummation. First, God promised Abraham that He would multiply his seed as the stars of the heaven and also as the sand which is upon the seashore (Gen. 22:17). Abraham had two kinds of descendants—the heavenly ones, which are the believers, the regenerated ones, and the earthly ones, the natural Jews who were born of the race of Abraham without being regenerated. The Jews are the earthly descendants of Abraham like the sand which is upon the seashore. But we are the heavenly descendants of Abraham, the stars of the heaven. Daniel 12:3 also indicates that the heavenly descendants of Abraham will be like the shining stars. The mentioning of the stars in Revelation 1 is a consummation indicating that all the messengers, the leading ones, of the churches should be altogether in the heavens. The stars are not only heavenly, but they are also in the heavens. This again is a consummation.

The Tree of Life

We can also see the consummation of other items in the seven epistles to the churches in Revelation 2 and 3. The first consummation is the tree of life. In the epistle to Ephesus the Lord says, "To him who overcomes, to him I will give to eat of the tree of life, which is in the paradise of God" (2:7). This is nothing new, but this is the tree of life in consummation. In Genesis 2, the tree of life was presented to man in a general way, but in Revelation 2:7 the right to eat the tree of life has been restricted to the overcomers. The unbelievers and even the common believers have no right to eat the tree of life in Revelation 2:7. Only he who overcomes has the right to eat. This is the consummation, but it is still not the ultimate consummation. We see the ultimate consummation of the tree of life in Revelation 22:2 and 14 where all the believers, not only the overcomers, will have the right to the tree of life in the new heaven and the new earth. The right to the tree of life there is based upon only one requirement—to have your robes washed, to be saved. In Revelation 2:7, however, the right to the tree of life is restricted to the overcoming ones who do not merely have their robes washed but have overcome the degraded church situation.

Balaam and Jezebel

In these epistles to the seven churches we also see Balaam (2:14) and Jezebel (2:20) and their consummation. Seemingly, these two are not related to life, to Christ, to the Spirit, or to the church. What they did, however, had very much to do, negatively, with the churches. Balaam did many things to distract God's people (Deut. 23:4; Num. 31:16; cf. 25:1-3) and Jezebel did many things to lead God's people astray (1 Kings 16:31; 19:2; 21:23, 25-26; 2 Kings 9:7). Throughout the centuries there have been many Balaams who distracted God's people and many Jezebels who mislead God's people.

The Hidden Manna

In Revelation 2:17 we also see the hidden manna, which again is only for a restricted number of people—the overcomers. In John 6 the Lord Jesus referred to manna: "I am the bread of life. Your fathers ate the manna in the wilderness, and they died. This is the bread which comes down out of heaven, that anyone may eat of it and not die" (vv. 48-50). In Revelation 2 the manna is applied again in a restricted way. This is the hidden manna in the ark of the testimony within the Holy of Holies. We can see again that there is nearly nothing new in the book of Revelation. All the items are in their consummation.

The Morning Star

The "Star out of Jacob" (Num. 24:17) and the star appearing at the Lord's birth (Matt. 2:7, 9-10) consummates in the morning star in Revelation 2:28. No star is as bright as the morning star. At His second appearing, Christ will be the morning star to His overcomers who watch for His coming. To all the others, He will appear only as the sun (Mal. 4:2).

The Pillar

In the seven epistles we also see the pillar in the temple (3:12). For us to realize the significance of the pillar in Revelation 3 we need to study 1 Kings 7:13-23. In the temple in the Old Testament there were two pillars. One was named Jachin and the other was named Boaz (v. 21). We also need to study the pillars in the church in Galatians 2:9 and the church being the pillar of the truth in 1 Timothy 3:15. The pillar mentioned in Revelation 3 is a consummation of the pillars in all these portions of the Word.

A Feast

Then to the church in Laodicea the promise to the overcomers is a feast (3:20). Based upon this thought of a feast, it is necessary to go back and study all the feasts in the Old Testament. There were three major feasts a year in the Old Testament (Deut. 16:16)—the feast of Unleavened Bread (Lev. 23:4-8), the feast of weeks (Deut. 16:10), which was also called the feast of Harvest (Exo. 23:16) or Pentecost (Lev. 23:15-22), and the feast of Tabernacles (Lev. 23:33-44). This shows us that the thought of a feast is not new in the book of Revelation. This thought was in the Old Testament already.

The Throne

In Revelation 4 we see the throne in its consummation (vv. 2-3). Ezekiel also saw the throne (Ezek. 1:26; 10:1). The throne of God revealed in Revelation is nearly the same as the portrait of the throne of God in Ezekiel. Daniel also saw the throne (Dan. 7:9). He saw a little concerning the throne and Ezekiel saw more, but neither of them saw as much as John did in Revelation. The throne in Revelation is not new, but it is a consummation of the throne. Seventeen chapters in the book of Revelation give us a record of this throne, from chapter four through chapter twenty. Out of this throne come the seven seals, the seven trumpets, and the seven bowls.

The Lamb

Then in the book of Revelation we see the Lamb. This is also a consummation. The Lamb is implied in the firstlings of the flock offered by Abel in Genesis 4:4. The Lamb was revealed in Genesis 22 with Abraham (vv. 7-8, 13). The ram offered by Abraham as a substitutionary sacrifice for Isaac points to the Lamb of God who takes away the sin of the world in John's writings. To understand the Lamb and its consummation in Revelation, it is necessary to go back to all the books of the Bible to see the Lamb. The Lion of the tribe of Judah (Rev. 5:5), undoubtedly, is the consummation of the Lion in Genesis 49:9. The redeeming Lamb (5:6) and the overcoming Lion are consummations. In redeeming, Christ has overcome all the negative things, especially the main enemy, Satan. He is the Lion-Lamb, accomplishing redemption by overcoming all the negative things. This is the consummation in chapter five. The ultimate consummation of the Lamb, though, is in chapter twenty-one. There we see the Lamb as the one who holds God within Him as light because the Lamb is the lamp and God is the light in the lamp (21:23). This indicates that Christ as the overcoming Redeemer holds God within Him. This is the ultimate consummation of the Lamb.

The Altar

When the fifth seal is opened in Revelation 6:9, we see

the altar. Underneath the altar are the souls of the martyred saints who cry out to God from Paradise for vengeance. This altar is not the altar within the tabernacle, the incense altar, but the altar in the outer court, the altar of burnt offering, where people offer things for God's satisfaction. The souls of the martyrs underneath the altar indicate that they were sacrifices offered to God on the altar for God's satisfaction.

The Seven Seals

Another item in the book of Revelation is the seven seals (5:1). The seal was also an item that was in the Old Testament (Dan. 9:24; 12:4). Something that is sealed means that it is kept secret and confidential. In the New Testament, in Revelation, is the consummation of the seals. These seals are the secrets of the entire universal administration of God.

The Seven Trumpets

In the book of Revelation we also see the seven trumpets, which are the execution of God's economy (8:6- 11:19). The trumpet is another item that was in the Old Testament. A trumpet was always used to indicate the move of God's people (Num. 10:2), especially the move in war (Josh. 6:5). Actually, the seven trumpets are soundings to the church to move on, to fight God's battle. Even the trumpets in Revelation are a consummation.

The Two Altars

In Revelation 8 we see Christ as the Priest burning the incense with the fire from the altar of burnt offering (vv. 3- 5). Christ came and stood at the altar of burnt offering (Exo. 27: 1-8) to get the fire. Then He burned the incense and offered it at the incense altar. These two altars are consummations. We must see that these are not the altars in type, but these are the real altars. The burnt offering altar surely cannot be in the heavens, but must be something on this earth. Also, Christ stood by this altar. As we have seen, the incense altar, undoubtedly, was in the heavenly tabernacle, but where is the altar on this earth? This shows us that to interpret the Bible is not an easy task. Actually, the earthly altar is a sign of the cross. The cross was not something accomplished in the heavens, but on earth. Therefore, when Christ stood by the altar of the offerings, this indicates Christ stood by His cross to get the fire from the cross to burn the incense to offer to God on the incense altar in the heavens.

All of these items need our study and need many messages to develop. In the next chapter we will continue to see more of the book of Revelation as a consummation of all the items related to Christ, life, the Spirit, and the church.

CHAPTER ELEVEN

THE VISION CONCERNING THE NEW JERUSALEM— THE ULTIMATE CONSUMMATION

(7)

REVELATION—A BOOK OF CONSUMMATION (PART 2)

In this chapter we will continue our fellowship on the consummation of all the items in the Bible related to Christ, the Spirit, life, and the church in the book of Revelation. In the previous chapter we ended with the brass altar, the altar of the offerings, and the golden altar, the altar of incense, in Revelation 8. Now we must see the temple of God which is in heaven (11:19) and the heavenly tabernacle (15:5).

The Temple of God

The heavens were opened to John and he saw the temple of God which is in heaven. In the temple was the ark of His covenant. We must say that there is a temple in the heavens because John saw it, and in that temple was the ark of testimony. Paul also told us in Hebrews 9 of the heavenly tabernacle (vv. 11, 24). Now we must ask whether or not there was a tabernacle in the heavens and a temple in the heavens at the same time. In the Old Testament these two did not exist at the same time. The tabernacle existed as a precursor to the temple, and the temple stood as a fulfillment of the tabernacle or a replacement. The tabernacle became the temple. Why then does the Bible tell us that in the New Testament there is the heavenly tabernacle and also the temple in heaven?

We must see that when the old covenant was made, it

was made by the sprinkled blood of the atonement. This blood was sprinkled on the tabernacle, not on the temple. Hebrews 9 tells us that this was a type (vv. 18-23). The earthly tabernacle was a type of the heavenly, and the earthly tabernacle was sprinkled with the blood of animal sacrifices for the enacting of the old covenant. Then to enact the new covenant we see in Hebrews 9 that the Lord Jesus used His own blood to sprinkle the heavenly tabernacle, which is the real tabernacle in the heavens. In Revelation 11, however, we do not see a tabernacle in the heavens but a temple because in Revelation it is not a matter of the enacting of a covenant but of the execution of God's government. Actually, therefore, these two do not exist simultaneously. The tabernacle was for the enacting of the covenant but in Revelation 11 we see a further stage—the temple for the execution of God's government. In Exodus the tabernacle was for the enacting of the old covenant, but it became the temple in 1 Kings 8 because by that time there was a king to execute God's government. In the New Testament in Hebrews 9 it is the tabernacle for the enacting of the new covenant. Then in Revelation it is the temple for God's execution of His kingdom.

The Tabernacle—Heaven Itself

At this point, we must look at Hebrews 9:24 carefully: "For Christ did not enter into the holy places made by hand, which are figures of the true, but into heaven itself." Here is a strong verse which tells us that heaven itself is the tabernacle. This does not mean that within the heavens there is a tabernacle. The tabernacle is heaven itself. The reflexive pronoun "itself" is inserted to strengthen the thought that the heavenly tabernacle is heaven itself.

Hebrews 9:1 says, "Then indeed the first covenant had ordinances of service, and its sanctuary, a sanctuary of this world." The sanctuary in this verse is the entire tabernacle (Exo. 25:8-9). Then Hebrews 9:11 says, "But Christ having come a High Priest of the good things that have come, through the greater and more perfect tabernacle not made by hand, that is, not of this creation." "This creation" means the earth, a part of the creation. The earth to us is "this creation," but another part of the creation is the heavens. All these verses show us that the heavenly tabernacle is heaven itself.

The translators of the Chinese version of the Bible translated "heaven itself" in Hebrews 9:24 into "heavenly mansion." They also translated "heaven" in 1 Peter 3:22 into "heavenly mansion." This actually is a Buddhistic translation because the Chinese term for heavenly mansion is a term used by Buddhism for a happy place. The Chinese version of the Bible in these verses has actually brought in a Buddhistic thought with a Buddhistic term. The Greek text of the Bible clearly uses two words in Hebrews 9:24—"heaven itself." Again we must see that the heavenly tabernacle is not something within the heavens just as the earthly tabernacle is something on earth, but the heavenly tabernacle is heaven itself. Such a wrong translation based upon a Buddhistic thought is misleading people.

Revelation 11:19 and 15:5

Now we must read Revelation 11:19: "And the temple of God which is in heaven was opened, and the ark of His covenant was seen in His temple." This verse, however, says clearly that the temple of God is in heaven. This surely is God's dwelling place in heaven. The word for temple in Greek in this verse is *naos*, the inner temple. The throne with the rainbow in 4:2-3 is the center of all the judgments executed over the earth in chapters six through eleven, on the negative side; whereas "the temple" with "the ark" is the center of all God's accomplishments in the universe carried out in chapters twelve through twenty-two, on the positive side. The throne is the center of God's administration before chapter eleven. Then from chapter twelve the center of God's government is no longer the throne but the temple with the testimony, the ark. Revelation 11:19 is continued by Revelation 15:5 which says, "And after these things I saw, and the temple of the tabernacle of the testimony in heaven was opened." In this verse we see the temple of the tabernacle. Therefore, the tabernacle is the heavens and the temple is the inner sanctuary. This inner sanctuary is the Holy of Holies where the ark is.

We also see in Revelation 21:10 that the New Jerusalem, considered by some others as the heavenly mansion, comes down out of heaven. Is this temple in Revelation 11:19 and 15:5 the heavenly mansion? Many Christians might say that this is the heavenly mansion, God's dwelling place, which descends out of heaven in Revelation 21:10. John, however, said that he saw no temple in the New Jerusalem because its temple is God and the Lamb (21:22). We must remember, though, that the New Jerusalem is the ultimate consummation of the tabernacle and of the temple in the Bible. The New Jerusalem is also called the tabernacle of God in Revelation 21:3.

First, in Hebrews 9:24 we saw that the heavenly tabernacle is heaven itself. Then in Revelation 11:19 and 15:5 we saw that in this tabernacle, which is heaven itself, is the temple of God, the Holy of Holies, within which is the ark. Revelation tells us, though, that the New Jerusalem, the tabernacle of God, comes down out of heaven. Does this mean that the entire heaven comes down? The entire heaven could not come down because the tabernacle of God comes down out of heaven. We also saw that in the New Testament there is first the tabernacle for the enacting of the new covenant, and then there is the temple to replace the tabernacle for God's administration. In Revelation 21, though, the tabernacle as the New Jerusalem is without the temple because God and the Lamb Himself are the temple.

The New Jerusalem—A Particular Item

My burden in pointing out these things is to show you that all these complications indicate one thing—that the New Jerusalem is a particular item which has nothing to do with the earthly tabernacle and the temple in the Old Testament. The New Jerusalem is not the tabernacle and the temple on this earth, nor is it the tabernacle and the temple in the heavens in Revelation 11:19 and 15:5. Many would interpret the passages in Revelation to mean that there is a temple in the heavens which eventually comes down out of heaven to be the New Jerusalem. Therefore, according to this interpretation the New Jerusalem is a physical dwelling place to God, just as the temple in heaven is. These complications, though, indicate that the New Jerusalem is neither the heavenly tabernacle nor the temple in heaven. Some may ask, "After the New Jerusalem comes down out of heaven, where did the heavenly tabernacle go?" My answer is that the heavenly tabernacle is heaven itself. When the New Jerusalem, God's eternal tabernacle, comes down out of heaven, heaven is left there as it is.

Then others might ask, "Where is the temple in the heavens when the New Jerusalem descends?" My answer to this is that I do not know. We know from history that the temple in the Old Testament was destroyed, but the Bible does not tell us where the temple in heaven will go. The New Jerusalem cannot be the temple in heaven in Revelation 11:19 and 15:5 because in the New Jerusalem John saw no temple (21:22). According to some people's concept, the New Jerusalem is a temple and God and the Lamb are another temple. Then there would be two temples—a temple within a temple. Actually, though, God and the Lamb are the temple and this temple is the New Jerusalem. This is not the temple in heaven in chapters eleven and fifteen but a new temple, a particular temple. The temple in heaven surely was not God Himself, but this temple is God and the Lamb Himself.

By this we can see that the New Jerusalem was not the tabernacle and the temple of the Old Testament on the earth. The New Jerusalem is not even the heavenly tabernacle (15:5) nor is it the temple in the heavens (11:19; 15:5). Let us summarize our two reasons for saying this:

1) In Hebrews 9:24 is a heavenly tabernacle, but this verse also tells us clearly that this heavenly tabernacle is heaven itself. The New Jerusalem is called the tabernacle of God in Revelation; this is not, however, the heavenly tabernacle because the heavenly tabernacle is heaven itself, but the New Jerusalem comes down out of heaven.

2) In Revelation 11:19 and 15:5 is a temple in heaven. Then when the New Jerusalem came, John said he saw no temple in it because now the temple is God and the Lamb Himself. This indicates that this temple, the New Jerusalem, is not that temple in heaven. John told us that the temple he saw was not physical and not a place, but personal. This temple is a Person, God and the Lamb, but the temple in heaven surely is a place.

This strongly proves that the New Jerusalem is altogether a new thing apart from the tabernacle and the temple both on earth and in heaven. The temple in heaven in 11:19 and 15:5 is not in the holy city. In this city is the new temple—God and the Lamb Himself. This New Jerusalem as God's tabernacle is God and the Lamb Himself as the temple. It is a particular tabernacle and a particular temple.

The Ultimate Consummation
of the Tabernacle and the Temple

The New Jerusalem is the ultimate consummation of

the tabernacle and the temple in the Bible. We have seen that the New Jerusalem as the tabernacle of God is God and the Lamb Himself as the temple. The New Jerusalem is not something physical but personal. Even in the New Testament the Lord Jesus as the tabernacle (John 1:14) is not a physical item, but a person. Also, the temple in the New Testament is firstly the Lord Jesus (John 2:19-21) and then the church (1 Cor. 3:16-17). The Lord Jesus and the church are not physical matters, but both are personal. The temple in the heavens surely is not personal, but the New Jerusalem as the temple will be God and the Lamb Himself, which is something personal. This means that the New Jerusalem is not the ultimate consummation of the Old Testament tabernacle and temple but the ultimate consummation of the New Testament tabernacle and temple, which are Christ and the church. This New Jerusalem is neither the heavenly tabernacle which is heaven itself nor the temple in heaven which is a place.

We must see three sets of the tabernacle and the temple: 1.) One set is in the Old Testament. The tabernacle and the temple here were physical and were types. 2.) Another set is the New Testament tabernacle and temple. This set is not physical but personal—Christ and the church. 3.) The third set is the heavenly tabernacle and the temple in heaven. Finally, the New Jerusalem is the ultimate consummation of the tabernacle and of the temple. It is neither the ultimate consummation of the set on earth in the Old Testament, nor of the set in the heavens in the New Testament. The New Jerusalem is the ultimate consummation of the set of Christ as the tabernacle and Christ and the church as the temple in the New Testament. It is the ultimate consummation, the full development, of the tabernacle which was Christ and of the temple which was both Christ and the church. Now the New Jerusalem is the ultimate consummation in full of Christ and of the church as God's eternal dwelling place and as our eternal dwelling place.

In the universe, before Moses, God had a dwelling place in heaven, and heaven, according to Hebrews 9:24, was God's tabernacle. The tabernacle was heaven itself and in that heavenly tabernacle was a spot where God stayed. This spot was the temple as the Holy of Holies of the heavenly tabernacle. This was the tabernacle with the temple as the Holy of Holies with the ark in it. When God charged Moses to build the tabernacle, He charged him to build it according to God's heavenly pattern (Heb. 8:5). Therefore, the tabernacle built by Moses and the temple built by Solomon in the Old Testament were according to the heavenly tabernacle and the temple in heaven. One set in the heavens was real and one set on the earth was a copy. The Old Testament tabernacle and temple was an earthly copy of the heavenly tabernacle and the temple in heaven. This copy was a shadow of Christ and the church as God's tabernacle and God's temple in the New Testament on this earth. The New Testament set of Christ and the church will consummate in the New Jerusalem. Therefore, the New Jerusalem is neither the set of the tabernacle and the temple in the heavens nor the set on earth in the Old Testament, but the continuation and even the consummation of the set in the New Testament of Christ and the church.

The Need to Purge Out the Leaven

We need to study the Bible in this way to purge out the leaven and to clear up the cloud that we may see God's New Testament economy and the New Testament ministry. This is the ministry which ministers the Triune God to produce the church and which will consummate in the New Jerusalem. We must realize that this ultimate consummation has been leavened and has been changed in every way in its intrinsic essence and element. It is not a small thing to fight against this leaven. This is the greatest leaven which the woman took and put into the biblical fine flour (Matt. 13:33). By His mercy, we must do our best to purge out this leaven.

Now we all should be able to see that the house in John 14 and the city in Revelation 21 are the ultimate consummation of Christ and the church. The truth concerning the house in John 14 and the city in Revelation 21 has been leavened and this leaven in the past centuries has governed the Christian teachings; therefore, so many have been robbed, misled, distracted, frustrated, and held back. Now we are ministering the genuine thing of God's economy. We must purge out this leaven. This is a big battle. All the items of these truths must be purely presented to the Christian public. If the house in John 14 and the city in Revelation 21 were physical things, they would have nothing to do with the Triune God working Himself into our being. Such a wrong interpretation is off of the line of the New Testament revelation.

The New Testament Revelation

The New Testament revelation shows us the Triune God and how He has gone through the processes to become the all-inclusive, life-giving Spirit to work Himself into us to become our life, our life supply, and our everything. Such a dispensing of the Triune God into His chosen and redeemed people will consummate in the New Jerusalem, which is a mutual dwelling place for Him and for His redeemed ones. This is the basic line of the New Testament revelation according to God's entire economy. To interpret the house in John and the city in Revelation as physical things would mean that they have nothing to do with the basic line of the New Testament revelation. This interpretation eventually robs the riches of the divine revelation and annuls all the proper principles of Biblical interpretation, so we lose everything. The heart and the pulse of the New Testament ministry is lost, is gone. The house in John and the city in Revelation must be brought back to their rightful position in God's New Testament economy. Both are the very illustration of the Triune God working Himself into our being to be the house and to be the city. In the house and in the city the divine Trinity is fully portrayed.

John 14 through 17 is a great section of the New Testament telling us the details concerning the Triune God dispensing Himself in His divine Trinity into our entire being. The ultimate consummation of the Triune God dispensing Himself into our being is this holy city, the New Jerusalem. This is not merely an interpretation of the Bible. What we have shared is very basic and very crucial. The Triune God is being dispensed into us to produce the house and to produce the city. The house is the result of the Triune God's dispensing and the city is the consummation of this result.

THE VISION CONCERNING THE NEW JERUSALEM— THE ULTIMATE CONSUMMATION

(8)

REVELATION—A BOOK OF CONSUMMATION (PART 3)

In this chapter we want to see the remaining items which are consummated in the book of Revelation, which is itself a book of consummation. We must remember that only the items which are related either indirectly or directly to Christ, the Spirit, life, and the church are consummated in this book.

The Universal Woman with Her Manchild

In chapter twelve is the universal woman with her manchild (vv. 1-2). Concerning this universal woman, it is necessary to study the positive females in the Old Testament beginning from Eve. Females such as Sarah and Rebecca should be included in your study. Also, even in the Old Testament God considered His chosen people as a female and furthermore as His counterpart, His wife (Isa. 54:5; 62:5; Jer. 2:2; 3:1, 14; 31:32; Ezek. 16:8; 23:5; Hosea 2:7, 19). This universal woman in Revelation 12 is a universal composition of all God's redeemed people, who have been portrayed as females. Isaiah 7:14 is another Old Testament passage alluding to this universal woman: "Therefore the Lord himself shall give you a sign; Behold, a virgin shall conceive, and bear a son, and shall call his name Immanuel." In the New Testament, of course, the church is considered as a female, as the wife of Christ (Eph. 5:23-25), as a pure virgin to Christ (2 Cor. 11:2), and even the believers themselves are considered as virgins (Rev. 14:4; S. S. 1:3). All this needs our study. Then you have a consummation in this universal woman. The seed of this woman, the manchild, also needs our study. The seed of the woman in Genesis 3:15, the seed of Abraham (Gal. 3:16), the seed of David (Rom. 1:3), and the seed of the virgin Mary are items which need to be included in our study. This manchild in Revelation 12 represents the stronger part of God's chosen people. This is a consummation.

The Great Red Dragon

The great red dragon is the consummation of the old serpent (Rev. 12:3, 9). In Genesis 3, Satan was a serpent, a smaller creature. Here in Revelation 12 he has become a dragon, much greater than a serpent. Hence, he is called "a great red dragon." "Red" here signifies the shedding of blood caused by Satan's murders (John 8:44).

The Beasts

In Revelation 13:1-2 is the coming beast "out of the sea," signifying the coming Caesar of the coming Roman Empire. This is the consummation of the four beasts in Daniel 7. This last beast in Revelation 13 is the ultimate one, the greatest one. Also, in Revelation 13 is another beast "out of the earth" who "had two horns like a lamb, and he spoke as a dragon" (v. 11). This is the false prophet who is the consummation of all the false prophets.

The Firstfruit and the Harvest

In Revelation 14:4 is the firstfruit, signifying the living overcomers among God's living people and in 14:15 is the harvest, signifying God's living people. To fully understand this consummation it is necessary to study Leviticus 23:9-14, a record of the feast of the firstfruits. The harvest is also recorded in Leviticus 23:15-22. Pentecost was the fulfillment of the feast of weeks (Deut. 16:10), which was also called the feast of harvest (Exo. 23:16), counting from the day of offering a sheaf of the firstfruits of the harvest unto the morrow after the seventh sabbath (Lev. 23:10-11, 15-16). This harvest affords God's people the way to have a feast of tabernacles (Lev. 23:33-44).

The Glassy Sea

In Revelation 15:2 is the glassy sea, which is a consummation of all the different baptisms in the Old and New Testaments. This includes the types of baptism in the Old Testament such as the flood which Noah passed through (1 Pet. 3:20-21) and the Red Sea as a baptism to the children of Israel (1 Cor. 10:1-2). Then with the tabernacle is the laver (Exo. 30:18). In the temple in 1 Kings 7 this laver became a great molten sea standing upon twelve oxen and accompanied with some small lavers (vv. 23-25, 38, 43-44). Then in the New Testament is the baptism of John, the baptism of Jesus and His disciples, and the baptism into the Triune God, into Christ, into the death of Christ, and into the Body of Christ. The glassy sea is a consummation of all the washings through the baptisms. We must realize that the ultimate consummation of all the baptisms will be the glassy sea in Revelation 15. Inside this glassy sea is not water but fire. Eventually, this glassy sea will be restricted into a lake, the lake of fire (Rev. 20:14-15). In the ultimate consummation the glassy sea was not enlarged but restricted. The sea will become a lake, which is smaller than a sea in its limitation. This shows God's mercy. In Revelation there is such an ultimate consummation of a negative item. All of this is quite meaningful.

Babylon the Great

In Revelation 17:5 is Babylon the Great, signifying the Roman Church. To understand this consummation you must study Babel in Genesis 11:1-9 and you must study the history of Babylon in the Old Testament. Babylon sent its army to destroy the holy city and was an opponent to Jerusalem (Jer. 39:1-3).

The Bride and the Wedding

After the great Babylon with its religious aspect in chapter seventeen and its material aspect in chapter eighteen is the wife of the Lamb, the Bride, in Revelation 19:7, signifying all the overcomers among God's redeemed people. This is also a consummation, as well as the wedding in 19:7-9. This wedding is a consummation of all the positive marriages in the Old and New Testaments.

An Army

After the wedding this wife will become an army (19:14). This army is also mentioned in Revelation 17:14. The heavenly army is an ultimate consummation of all the people who have been fighting for God's interests through the generations.

The Millennial Kingdom

Then in Revelation 20:4-6 is the millennial kingdom. In the millennial kingdom the saints in the manifestation of the kingdom of the heavens will be the kings. This is the heavenly part of the millennium. The earthly part of the millennium includes the kingdom of the Messiah (2 Sam. 7:13), the tabernacle of David (Acts 15:16), the kingdom of the Son of Man (Matt. 13:41; Rev. 11:15). This is the consummation of the kingdom of God.

The New Jerusalem

The greatest consummation is the New Jerusalem. The New Jerusalem is an ultimate and all-inclusive consummation of nearly all the positive things both in the Old Testament and in the New Testament. In this ultimate consummation is the tree of life, which was mentioned in

Genesis 2:9. In this city we also see pearls, which are the consummation of the bdellium in Genesis 2:12 and of the pearl in Matthew 13:45-46. Many items in the New Jerusalem can be traced throughout the entire Bible. Also, many items in this consummation are consummations of items in the Gospel of John. In the Gospel of John is the tree of life typified by the vine tree in John 15. There are also rivers of living water mentioned in John 7:38. There is the light of life in John 8:12. John 1:4 says, "In Him was life, and the life was the light of men." What is mentioned or revealed in the Gospel of John will consummate in the New Jerusalem.

In the New Jerusalem we also see the all-inclusive and practical consummation of the divine Trinity. I have mentioned already that John 14 through 17 is the greatest section on the Trinity in the Bible. The divine Trinity is revealed in these chapters, not in a doctrinal way, but in a way of being wrought into the believers in Christ. This dispensing of the divine Trinity into the believers in Christ will consummate in the New Jerusalem.

The Spirit and the Bride

Finally, Revelation 22:17 says, "The Spirit and the bride say...." This verse does not tell us that the bridegroom and the bride speak together, but that the Spirit and the bride speak together. This is the consummation of what John the Baptist told his disciples in John 3:29: "He who has the bride is the bridegroom." The end of the New Testament eventually reveals to us that it is not Christ as the Bridegroom to have the bride but the Spirit— "The Spirit and the bride say...." This very Spirit is the all-inclusive, life-giving Spirit as the consummation of the processed Triune God. This Spirit is the very Bridegroom who was Christ in the Gospel of John and who was also the Husband in Revelation 21 (vv. 2, 9). In Revelation 22 the Bridegroom is the Spirit, who in chapters two and three was the Spirit speaking to the churches.

THE NEED OF A VISION TO PRESERVE US

We must see all these things because we have been covered, veiled, leavened, distracted, held back, misled, delayed, and frustrated. Without a clear vision we cannot be rescued. We need such a strong vision to take away the veil, to purge out the leaven, and to bring us back to the central lane. Such a vision will control us, preserve us, and keep us in the proper, genuine oneness. It will also direct us, lead us, and bring us on the right lane to the right goal. If we do not have a clear vision concerning the house in John 14 and especially a clear vision concerning the city in Revelation 21 and 22, I do not believe we could be fully kept in the proper line of life. It would be impossible to unify the many teachings among us in order to keep the oneness. No one can control what others teach. Everybody has the liberty and right to teach what they want. No one can control us. If you were not allowed to teach a certain way, you could go somewhere else. Let us suppose that you did not go away, but that we all stayed together. Although we are together, let us suppose that you teach what you teach, I teach what I teach, and another teaches what he teaches. If this were the case, this would not be oneness. At the very least it is a scattering. Eventually this scattering would become a dividing. Therefore, the only thing that can preserve us and keep us in the genuine, not human made, oneness is to see this vision.

I must testify that by the Lord's mercy I have been preserved over more than fifty years, not by anyone controlling me, but by seeing this vision. I cannot teach anything else. This vision has spoiled me concerning the teaching of other doctrines. I possibly could have made a name for myself in teaching typology, prophecy, and dispensation. I studied these things for seven and a half years. These were the best years of my entire life, from the age of twenty to the age of twenty-eight. These years are the top years for a young person to learn things. These things that I have learned are still useful. In my interpretation of the types in Exodus, I did not spend much time to write the outlines for the messages since I received the basic help in interpreting these types when I was in the golden time of my life. I dropped all these things many years ago, but when the need arose I still could interpret these types. If I had not been "distracted" by the New Testament ministry and if I had continued preaching typology, prophecy, and dispensation, I could have been an expert in these areas, especially in China. Instead, I dropped these things. Who told me to drop them? No one asked me. I was controlled by this heavenly vision. I believe that even the angels can testify that I was thoroughly, fully, and absolutely one with Brother Watchman Nee's ministry. What caused me to be one with his ministry? Nothing but this vision. Some people are now spoiling Brother Nee's name. I do not care what they did or what they are doing. I can never deny that Brother Nee took the lead to take this ministry toward this way, and I saw it and followed him one hundred percent. We all have been preserved.

OUR MINISTRY

We must learn by His mercy to seek after this seeing of the vision. We must see this. Then we all will be like the early apostles who did not minister anything but this one, unique, New Testament economy. Of course, they covered a lot of items. Paul taught something concerning head covering (1 Cor. 11:2-16), but he did it in the scope of the dispensing of the Triune God. Even head covering was taught by the Apostle under this view and in this scope. Paul did not teach anything apart from the New Testament economy, which is the dispensing of the divine Trinity into all of God's chosen, redeemed, and regenerated people. We must see this. We should not teach anything with the motive of attracting a crowd by stirring up people's interest. Our ministry is not to get a crowd; it is not to get a market for our work; it is not to stir up people's interest.

Our ministry is to minister the Triune God according to
His eternal economy and by His New Testament ministry.

We cannot deny that the Lord has shown us something
over this past half century. You all can testify that once
you touch the publication of the Lord's New Testament
ministry, you can sense a particular flavor. It is something
particular in its divine nature of the New Testament
ministry. Brothers, if you learn anything of this ministry,
you must learn this.

You must dive into all the things that the Lord has put
out in His recovery. If you would dive into these matters,
you would get educated and built up. To get thoroughly
educated humanly speaking, we must pass through six
years of elementary school, six years of junior high and
high school, and four years of college. After this study you
are qualified to do research. In like manner, I hope that all
of you would spend some time to dive into the holy Word
by the help that the Lord has given us throughout the past
sixty years. I have discovered that nearly all the things we
have published have remained on your bookshelf. You did
not get into all the crucial points. You still have not gotten
into many of the books of the Bible. This shows that you
are still in the old things.

I would like to take hymn 1348 as an example again.
Actually, this hymn was written by someone who is not
among us. Then it was brought in and used by us for a few
years. It was finally edited and put into the final edition of
our supplement. We all have sung this hymn for some
years, but no one realized that it was a foreign thing to us.
We were singing a hymn for the unbelievers. Although we
did not realize it, our singing of this hymn carries with it
the concept that we have never been regenerated, that we
will never be in the city, but always outside the city, that
we have no right to eat of the tree of life but could only
enjoy the leaves of the tree, and that we will still have
tears. Even though this is fully revealed in Revelation 21
and has clear subtitles in the Recovery Version, no one had

this kind of realization. We were in the training on the book of Revelation and had a review of that training, but everyone forgot. This is just one illustration. I could probably pick up fifty other points from the notes of the Recovery Version to check with you on other items of the truth, and probably not one of you would be able to answer me. The diamonds and the treasures are all here, yet we go to other sources to get something "precious," to get something different, strange, and new to catch people and to stir up people's interest. This is not the New Testament ministry. This is to teach differently, which is mentioned in 1 Timothy 1:3. Paul tells us in this verse that he left Timothy in Ephesus in order that he might charge certain ones not to teach differently. Paul also instructed him in verse 4 to charge these ones to take care of God's economy. Today we must be on the alert, not for others but for ourselves. Speaking for myself, I would not be unconsciously utilized and usurped by God's enemy to minister something such as "copper" which looks like gold but actually is not gold. God does not want copper. Copper must be judged. God wants gold to express Himself. Eventually, in the New Jerusalem there will be no copper; there will only be gold. We all must see such a thing.

I do not like to control anyone, I would never control anyone, and I have never been controlled by anybody. Even Brother Nee never controlled me. No one can control anything. However, in the Lord's recovery we all must see what the New Testament ministry is. Some people have said, "Brother Lee forces every church to study his Life-studies." Probably if they were me they would do this, but I would never do it. I would not force you to use the Life-studies, rather, if I came to know that you held this kind of concept, I would have the ministry office stop mailing any of my writings to you. However, as one brother who is a little older than you are and who is respected by you as your helper, I would say an honest word to you—if you miss the Lord's ministry in His recovery you miss a lot.

You suffer the loss, but for you alone to suffer the loss is a small thing. You and I personally mean nothing, but if we miss the Lord's ministry, we delay the Lord's recovery. This is a great thing.

You may say that you have never been negative toward the ministry. Many of you have never been negative, but your indifferent attitude without a sharp discernment of the truth and your lukewarmness did and still is bothering me. You need to be absolute. You need to be burning. You need to go on. Do not think that just because you have been under this training for years that you have gotten to know everything. I believe that in these recent days the Lord has shown us that we do not know that much. The New Testament ministry is a big field for us to explore and a big mine for us to dig in. We should not stop here.

The prayer meeting this morning (see chapter ten) was a strong illustration to me that we have not made much progress in the Lord's recovery. We have still remained very old. According to the burden in my spirit, this morning we should have come together to cry out to the Lord to rescue us from the traditional things, to have mercy upon us and give us grace that we might be brought into His New Testament ministry in a full way. Also, we should have prayed for the churches and for every saint in the recovery to be brought into such a full realization of the New Testament ministry. In our prayer, it was not necessary for us to repeat all the things that we had heard to give others a sermon. That was not our burden in coming together to pray. We need to come together to pour out our being, to cry to the Lord with weeping, "Lord, have mercy upon us. I have been in the recovery for years and I have never seen the things. Have mercy upon me. Have mercy upon all the churches. Have mercy upon all the Christians, Lord. Use us to enlighten them. Use us to present God's economy to them." We need to pray in this way. We do not need to pray doctrinally. My heart has been broken again and again by this kind of situation. I hope that you would weep with me. Many of us who are here need to weep for a few days. When I called a gathering last night for us to pray for half an hour, I meant that we should pray in this way. I did not mean for you all to come here to waste your time for thirty minutes. Again, this is a strong proof that we have not been brought into the real realization of the New Testament ministry.

THE VISION CONCERNING
THE NEW JERUSALEM—
THE ULTIMATE CONSUMMATION

(9)

A SUPERSTITIOUS CONCEPT

Many Christians still hold a superstitious concept concerning the so-called heavenly mansion; John 14:3 is their basis for believing that the Lord Jesus has gone to the heavens to prepare such a mansion for them. According to the King James version of the Bible verses 2 and 3 of John 14 say, "In my Father's house are many mansions: if it were not so, I would have told you. I go to prepare a place for you. And if I go and prepare a place for you, I will come again, and receive you unto myself; that where I am, there ye may be also." Based upon the King James rendering, many believe that the Lord has gone to prepare a heavenly mansion in the heavens. Then He will come again and will receive the believers to Himself that where He is they also may be.

The superstition is that for so many centuries many Christians preached and taught that once a believer dies he immediately goes to the heavenly mansion. However, many of them also believe that according to this verse once the heavenly mansion will be completed, the Lord will come back to receive the believer into this mansion. Even if we did believe that what is mentioned in 14:2 is the heavenly mansion, this verse does not indicate that immediately after we die we go into this mansion because 14:3 says the Lord will come again to receive us. These verses in John do not say that after we die we will go to the heavenly mansion. According to the Lord's word in 14:3 many Christians hold the concept that the Lord is now preparing the heavenly mansion and that after He is finished He will come back to receive the believers. If this is the case, then as long as the Lord is not here yet, this indicates that the heavenly mansion has not yet been completed. According to this interpretation of the Bible we must ask, "After a believer dies, where shall he go?" How can they go to the so-called heavenly mansion when it is not yet ready? This shows us the foolish, blind, nonsensical, superstition based upon these verses. In these verses the Lord does not say, "I am going to prepare a heavenly mansion. Then I will come back to receive you, but in case you die during the time I am preparing the mansion, you still may come to me. I am there waiting for you." The Lord only said that He would go to prepare a place and come again to receive the believers there. For centuries many Christians taught people using John 14:2-3 as a basis, especially at funerals. They read this portion and told people that the Lord has prepared a place in heaven. Nobody asked them, however, why the Lord had not come yet since He had already prepared a place. John 14:3 does not say that the believers go to the Lord, but it says that the Lord will come back to receive them to Himself.

Another portion of the Scriptures also tells us that at the Lord's coming back "the dead in Christ shall rise first; then we who are living, who remain, shall be caught up at the same time together with them in clouds into a meeting of the Lord in the air" (1 Thes. 4:16-17). This portion of the Word shows us clearly that the dead saints are not in the heavens because they will be raised up. If they had already gone to the heavens, then when the Lord comes back they would come with the Lord. This shows us that many Christians, including many Christian teachers, became drugged with this concept of the heavenly mansion. They did not consider the pure Word. Even J. N. Darby, in his *Synopsis of the Books of the Bible*, told people that the Lord was going to prepare a place and that we all would go there. We can see from this that Darby, who was called the king of the expositors, was also wrong in his interpretation of John 14:2-3.

PSALM 36:8-9

Let us read Psalm 36:8-9 to see something further: "They shall be abundantly satisfied with the fatness of thy house; and thou shalt make them drink of the river of thy pleasures. For with thee is the fountain of life: in thy light shall we see light." For many years I wondered how a house could have fatness. It is possible for edible things to have fatness. Chicken, fish, and cattle may have fatness. How could a house, though, have fatness? Psalm 36:8 says they shall be abundantly satisfied with the fatness of God's house. God's house does have the fatness, but what is the fatness? The definition of the word fatness according to the Hebrew dictionary of the *Strong's Concordance* is very interesting and meaningful. Strong's says that figuratively speaking fatness means abundance and specifically refers to the fatty ashes of sacrifices. The fatness of God's house comes from the sacrifices, the offerings. All the offerings in the Old Testament were types of the all-inclusive Christ; therefore, the fatness of God's house refers to the riches of Christ. All of the offerings are types of Christ and the fatty ashes of these offerings are the signs of His accomplishment. When you see the ashes of the offerings, they tell you that everything you need has been accomplished by Christ's death, by His being offered to God. Now we are here "enjoying these ashes." This is a figurative speaking of Christ being the rich sacrifices through His death, and this is the fatness of God's house. This verse also tells us that the Lord shall make us to drink of the river of His pleasures. The fatness refers to

Christ, and the river refers to the Spirit. Then verse 9 says, "For with thee is the fountain of life." This refers to God the Father as the source, as the fountain, not the spring. The fountain is the real source, while the spring is the springing up, the bubbling up, of the fountain. The fountain of life refers to the Father as the very source of life. Verse 9 continues to say, "In thy light shall we see light." Light also refers to the Father. The Father is not only the source of life but also the source of light. Life comes first and then light. This corresponds with John 1:4: "In Him was life, and the life was the light of men." Even in such a short portion of the Word in the poetry of the ancient psalmist we can see the divine Trinity. We can see Christ as the fatness, the Spirit as the river, and the Father as the source of life and light. This is marvelous!

Strictly speaking, in the Old Testament there was no grace yet. Grace had not yet been given because grace came through Jesus Christ (John 1:17). This Psalm shows us, however, that even in the dispensation of law some of the Old Testament saints who were seeking after God enjoyed the Trinity in the temple. They were abundantly satisfied with the fatness of God's house. In the temple of God, the ancient saints could participate in the enjoyment of the Triune God—the fatness of Christ, the living water of the Spirit, and the life and light of God the Father as the fountain. Today in the so-called church, today's Christendom, there is very little satisfaction with the fatness, drinking of the river of God's pleasures, and realization of the fountain of life and light. Many Christians talk about "the heavenly mansion" with no thought or no concept whatsoever concerning the satisfaction of the fatness, concerning the drinking of the living water, and concerning the fountain of life and of light. According to their concept, they merely have a bare heavenly mansion. When they talk about the New Jerusalem, they do not have the realization and they do not care for the fatness for satisfaction, the river of God's pleasures for His people's drinking, and the fountain of life and light. This is why when we come to John 14, we must look at the house according to the entire context of this chapter. If we would read chapters fourteen through seventeen of John by dropping the concept that the Father's house is the heavenly mansion, we would be able to see how much fatness is in these four chapters and what a river of God's pleasures is flowing there with God the Father as the fountain of life and light.

Many Christians only take verses 2 and 3 of John 14 to say that the Father's house is the heavenly mansion. They do not relate the rest of the four chapters (John 14—17) to these few verses. If they would relate this context to these verses, it would take away their traditional, human, natural, religious, and superstitious mentality. They would realize that the Father's house could not be a bare house, a heavenly mansion. It must be a house full of the fatness of Christ, a house where the living water is flowing, and a house where the fountain of life and light can be found. Today this is the church. In a proper church life there are the riches of Christ for your satisfaction, the flowing of the river to quench your thirst, and the fountain, a source of light and life. This is not only defined, described, offered, and presented in John 14 through 17, but it is also presented in all the Epistles. Paul's writings are filled with the fatness, the unsearchable riches of Christ. The river as the Spirit of life is richly flowing in the fourteen Epistles of Paul. Also, concerning the church life in Paul's Epistles one can discover and find a fountain of life and light. Then this house will consummate in the New Jerusalem. In the ultimate consummation we see exactly the same thing—the fatness, the river, and the fountain of life and light.

Even in the dispensation of law before the dispensation of the New Testament age, the seeking saints were enjoying the Triune God. They did not need to go to the heavens to enjoy Him, but they could and did enjoy the Triune God in His dwelling place on this earth. If this was the case with them, how much more should we then enjoy the Triune God in such a high way today in His dwelling place on this earth, the church. Where is the church? The church is where the fatness, the flowing river, and the fountain of life and light are. Some people may claim that they are the church. However, if there is no fatness of Christ, no flowing river of the Spirit, and no fountain of life and light, that is not the proper church. The proper church is a house where the fatness of Christ is satisfying people, where the Spirit flows as the river of God's pleasures, and where the fountain of life and light could be found. This is the church, not in heaven but on earth, and this will consummate in the New Jerusalem where the Triune God will be our enjoyment in the same way.

The Governing Vision

Some of you have been reading, studying, and reciting Psalm 36:8-9 for years, but you could not and did not interpret these verses in this way. The only way we could interpret these verses in this way is by the governing vision—the Triune God is working Himself into His chosen and redeemed people to be their life and life supply, to saturate their entire being with the divine Trinity, that is, with the Father as the fountain, the Son as the fatness, and the Spirit as the river. This is the vision that governs and directs you to interpret any portion of the Bible. Genesis, Exodus, or any book of the Bible must be interpreted by such a governing vision. Without such a vision, you may present a good message based upon Psalm 36:8-9, yet it will be so shallow, touching nothing of the divine Trinity. Even if you were to go to *Strong's Concordance* and discover that the fatness refers to the fatty ashes of the sacrifices, without such a vision you would never think that this refers to Christ. You must have the governing principle. Then when you see the word sacrifices, you would be so clear that this refers to the Second of the divine Trinity, Christ. Then it would also be easy for you to understand the river of God's pleasures. Without such a vision, it is not so easy to understand what this river is. Romans 14:17 refers back to this river when it tells us that the kingdom of God is "righteousness and peace and joy in the Holy Spirit." The joy in the Holy Spirit is the river of pleasures, or we could say the river of pleasures is the Spirit of joy. We must realize that the Bible was written under this governing principle. When we pick up this key, we can open up every part of the Bible. This principle helps us to interpret the fountain of life and "in thy light shall we see light" (Psalm 36:9). This principle helps us to see in John that life is in Him and that this life is the light of men (1:4). God is life and God is light. Therefore, He Himself is the fountain of both life and light.

Every book of the Bible confirms your understanding of this Scripture passage because the entire Bible was written according to the principle of the Triune God wrought into His redeemed people as their enjoyment, their drink, and their fountain of life and light. The application of this principle in interpreting any portion of the New Testament is endless. Then your message, using any portion, will be greatly enriched. It will be full of the fatness, full of the flowing of the river of pleasures, and full of the fountain of life and of light. Your message and your ministry will be different. There will be an intrinsic principle within and governing whatever you speak, teach, and preach. This is my burden. Merely to read the lines of a Life-study to pick up some points and titles for our message does not work. You have not been constituted with such a principle, and this principle has not become a vision to you. You may have the eyes to read the Bible and the mind to understand it, but you do not have the key to open it. You need the key.

Psalm 1 Versus Psalm 36

I would like to give some illustrations showing how to discern the interpretation of the Bible by such a key. Psalm 1:1-2 says, "Blessed is the man that walketh not in the counsel of the ungodly, nor standeth in the way of sinners, nor sitteth in the seat of the scornful. But his delight is in the law of the Lord; and in his law doth he meditate day and night." The person described here is quite wonderful. He stays away from anything evil, musing in the law of the Lord day and night. What, however, is the difference between this psalmist and the one in Psalm 36? The one in Psalm 1 is a working one, a behaving one, an acting one. This one is not an enjoying one. The psalmist in Psalm 36, though, was not musing in the law. He was not practicing not walking in the council of the ungodly, not standing in the way of sinners, and not sitting in the seat of the scornful. He was not in the law, but he was in the house enjoying the fatness, the river of pleasures, and the fountain of life and light. Verse 3 of Psalm 1 continues, "And he shall be like a tree planted by the rivers of water." To drink the river of God's pleasures is one thing and to be planted by the side of the river is another thing. Psalm 36 is according to the divine Trinity in God's economy, and Psalm 1 is according to religious ethics, according to the natural concept of religion. This is why we interpreted Psalm 1 for years, not on the positive side but on the negative side. Verses 4 and 5 of this Psalm say, "The ungodly are not so: but are like the chaff which the wind driveth away. Therefore the ungodly shall not stand in the judgment, nor sinners in the congregation of the righteous. For the Lord knoweth the way of the righteous: but the way of the ungodly shall perish." These verses are altogether religiously ethical and natural.

THE GOVERNING PRINCIPLE

We should thank the Lord that after Psalm 1 is Psalm 2. The conclusion of Psalm 2 is that all they that put their trust in Christ are blessed, and that we should "kiss the Son, lest he be angry" (v. 12). Do not meditate in the law but kiss the Son. (This is fully covered in chapter one of the book *Christ and the Church Revealed and Typified in the Psalms.*)

Most of the Bible expositors, if not all, appraised and uplifted Psalm 1. Why would we dare to say something different? What is the basis for our interpretation of these two Psalms? Again, our basis of interpretation is the principle of the vision of the Triune God being wrought into our being. This really makes a difference.

I do not care how young you are, how old you are, or how many years you have been in the Lord's service. If you are not possessed and captured by this vision, sooner or later your preaching, your teaching, and your messages will be somewhat natural. You will have no ability to discern what portion of the Bible is religious and what portion of the Bible is of life. During the training on the books of James and Mark many of you probably wondered how I could interpret the book of James in such a way. This is because I have the key of this basic principle. I say again that the Bible, the holy Word, was written under this governing principle. I believe that a number of the writers of the Scriptures did not realize this principle at the time they were writing because they were under the inspiration of the Holy Spirit. They were means, instruments, used by the Spirit. Undoubtedly, Paul knew and realized what he was writing, but I do not believe that some writers, such as those in the Old Testament, knew what the governing principle of their writings was. Some of them must have known that they were under the inspiration of the Holy Spirit. The reason why I say this is because David told us in 2 Samuel 23:2, "The Spirit of the Lord spake by me, and his word was in my tongue." David told us that he was under the inspiration of the Holy Spirit to compose a Psalm. Whether or not the writers of the Scriptures knew or did not know that they were under the inspiration of the Holy Spirit, we must realize that the "rudder" was in the hand of the Holy Spirit in their writing of the Scriptures (2 Peter 1:20-21).

The sequence of the Trinity in Psalm 36:8-9 is the same in Luke 15. In Luke 15 Christ is first as the

Shepherd (vv. 4-7), the Spirit is second as the seeking woman (vv. 8-10), and the Father is third (vv. 11-32). In Psalm 36:8-9 Christ is the fatness, the Spirit is the river, and the Father is the fountain. We should believe in Christ; then we receive the Spirit who leads us to the Father. We enjoy the fatness of Christ; then we have a share of the flowing Spirit; and then we are in the presence of the Father enjoying Him as the fountain of life and light. This indicates how the Old Testament, like the Psalms, was written by the Holy Spirit.

We must have the key, the governing principle of the writings in the Bible. Just as the master key to a building gives us the ability to open the door in that building, so we need the key to open every book of the Bible. This key also gives us the ability to discern every portion of the Scriptures. This vision, this principle, can be applied to every portion of the word in the Bible, including typology, prophecy, and even dispensations. As a young man fifty-five years ago, I spoke concerning typology, prophecies, and dispensations. Even though I spoke in an interesting way, I did not relate them to life at all. There was no life there. Today, however, if I would interpret any type it would be full of the enjoyment of Christ, the flowing of the river of the Spirit, and the fountain of life and light.

Every portion of the one hundred and twenty Life-study Messages of Genesis is filled with life, the river, the fatness, the riches of Christ, the flowing of the Spirit, and the fountain of the Father as life and light. This principle governs all the Life-study Messages. I have been much criticized for this. Some people say that it is not necessary to come and listen to me because I always preach and teach the same thing. I totally agree with this statement. What I serve is always "American beef." This beef is cooked and served by me in many ways; sometimes it is in the style of steak, sometimes in the style of a hamburger, and sometimes I serve this beef in the Chinese way of stewing. Whatever I serve is beef. Beef is my key and I have nothing but beef. What is this "beef"?—the processed Triune God. This is the beef. Some Chinese cooks boast that they have twenty ways to cook certain things. By the Lord's mercy, I can boast to these cooks that I have hundreds of ways to cook my "beef" because I have put out more than two thousand messages. Every message is a different way of cooking the same thing—the Triune God being wrought into His redeemed people. Also, all of the hymns I have written were written under the same governing principle. The biblical way is this way—the Triune God is "cooked" in different ways from the first page of Genesis to the last page of Revelation. This is the Bible. You need the key. If you have the key, you will eventually say that every page of the Bible is the same. For instance, all the females in the Bible are the same—Eve, Sarah, Rebeccah, and the seeking one in the Song of Songs are types. The ultimate consummation of these females in the Bible is the eternal wife, which is the very tabernacle. With this key and by this principle one can wrap up the entire Bible. Then we can discern whether or not someone else's teaching and ministering is holding people back or frustrating and distracting them.

A certain message may be wonderful, eloquent, and very inspiring, yet in principle that may be a distracting message, a holding back message. We could be laboring for ten years, but by one message people could be held back for five years. Still, most of the people who listen may appreciate that kind of message. To discern this, you need this basic principle of this vision to see that the Triune God is the very essence and should be the very essence of every message that we put out. Only this serves God's purpose, only this keeps us from being led astray, and only this can keep us in oneness from today through eternity.

In 1 Corinthians Paul charged the believers to speak the same thing (1:10) and in Philippians he charged them to think the same thing (2:2). Philippians is a book on the Triune God—specifically on Christ and specifically on the bountiful supply of the Spirit of Jesus Christ. When we are enjoying the bountiful supply of the Spirit of Jesus Christ, we have the key. In Philippians Paul tells us that he aspired to be found in Christ (3:9). If we can be found by others in nothing else but Christ, then we have the key. Not only will our messages be found in Christ, but also even our being, our person will be found in Christ. We are a person in Christ because we live Christ and we magnify Christ. Because we are a person in Christ, our speaking is the speaking in Christ and our message is a message in Christ. Everything is directed by this principle.